AN EXTRA SHOT
Wisdom For Everyday Life

CHIP KAWALSINGH
Foreword by John Partington

HARVEST
City Publishing
harvestcitypublishing.com

AN EXTRA SHOT
Wisdom For Everyday Life

CHIP KAWALSINGH
Foreword by John Partington

ISBN 978-0-9561415-2-1
A catalogue record for this book is available from the British Library

First published in the UK in 2010 by Harvest City Publishing
Printed by the MPG Books Group in the UK

Editing, design and layout by Darrell Woods
Original cover design by Jena Clark (www.jenaclark.com)
Additional editing by Paul Goffin, Nicola Holmes and Sarah Woods

Scripture References

Scripture taken from The Message. Copyright © 1993, 1994, 1995, 1996, 2000, 2001, 2002. Used by permission of
NavPress Publishing Group.

Scripture quotations marked NLT are taken from the Holy Bible, New Living Translation, copyright 1996, 2004.
Used by permission of Tyndale House Publishers, Inc., Wheaton, Illinois 60189. All rights reserved.

Scripture taken from the New King James Version. Copyright © 1982 by Thomas Nelson,Inc. Used by permission.
All rights reserved.

Scripture taken from the Contemporary English Version © 1995 by the American Bible Society. Used by
permission. All Rights Reserved.

Scripture taken from the Holy Bible, New International Version®. Copyright © 1973, 1978, 1984 International
Bible Society. Used by permission of Zondervan. All rights reserved.

Scripture quotations taken from the Amplified® Bible, Copyright © 1954, 1958, 1962, 1964, 1965, 1987 by The
Lockman Foundation. Used by permission. (www.Lockman.org)

Scripture quotations taken from the 21st Century King James Version®, copyright © 1994. Used by permission of
Deuel Enterprises, Inc., Gary, SD 57237. All rights reserved.

Scriptures and additional materials quoted are from the Good News Bible © 1994 published by the Bible
Societies/HarperCollins Publishers Ltd., UK Good News Bible © American Bible Society 1966, 1971, 1976,
1992. Used with permission.

Emphasis has been added to some scriptures by the author. Comments on scripture are
clearly indicated as such in the text.

www.harvestcitypublishing.com

DEDICATION

I would like to dedicate this book to my parents, Tony and Zenora Kawalsingh, who for many years provided me with all I needed for a foundation to make wise choices. I am forever grateful and indebted to them for this.

Also, to my parents-in-law, David and Margaret Glave, who passed on godly wisdom to my wife Sarah, who is now embedding this daily into our children.

And lastly to my wife, Sarah, and my boys, Brandon and Dylan. I love you all!

CONTENTS

FOREWORD

The Bible makes it abundantly clear that there is one matter that is of supreme importance – in fact, above all others.

Proverbs 4 says 'Get wisdom – wisdom is the principle thing!'

Having known Chip for a number of years now, and been both challenged and blessed by his preaching and writings, I am delighted to thoroughly recommend *An Extra Shot* to everyone.

The nuggets of truth contained within these pages are drawn from both personal experience and of course God's Word.

By reading, meditating and most importantly of all putting into practice the principles and wisdom contained in every chapter, the reader will be better equipped to live an abundant and purpose filled life.

John Partington
National Leader, Assemblies of God GB

An Extra Shot

PREFACE

I have written this book for the sole purpose of bringing you, the reader, closer to God. *An Extra Shot* is for seasoned believers as well as new or potential believers and has the importance of the local Church as an underlying thread within its thought and inspiration. Scriptures are placed specifically for quick access to God's Word, no matter where you are.

What Do I Need?

When reading this book it would be helpful to have the following (although they are not necessary!):

1. Pen or pencil. So you can record your God thoughts and what you feel the Holy Spirit is saying to you.
2. Your Bible. This is the greatest book ever!
3. A cup of coffee, tea or whatever drink you like! You don't need to set aside loads of spare time to get into *An Extra Shot*, just a few minutes whenever and wherever you are.

As you read these pages, I pray that you can connect with God and get an extra shot of wisdom for daily living. Enjoy!

Chip Kawalsingh

AN EXTRA SHOT
Wisdom For Everyday Life

(Chapter 1)

I Am Strong

2 Corinthians 6:3-10 (NLT)

We live in such a way that no one will stumble because of us, and no one will find fault with our ministry. In everything we do, we show that we are true ministers of God. We patiently endure troubles and hardships and calamities of every kind. We have been beaten, been put in prison, faced angry mobs, worked to exhaustion, endured sleepless nights, and gone without food. We prove ourselves by our purity, our understanding, our patience, our kindness, by the Holy Spirit within us and by our sincere love. We faithfully preach the truth. God's power is working in us. We use the weapons of righteousness in the right hand for attack and the left hand for defence. We serve God whether people honour us or despise us, whether they slander us or praise us. We are honest, but they call us impostors. We are ignored, even though we are well known. We live close to death, but we are still alive. We have been beaten, but we have not been killed. Our hearts ache, but we always have joy. We are poor, but we give spiritual riches to others. We own nothing, and yet we have everything.

Whenever I feel like life is getting on top of me, when things aren't going to plan, or when I feel exhausted and fed up, I read this passage and it brings everything back into perspective. The truth of the matter is this: we will all have troubles and hardships (John 16:33), but the key to overcoming is found in our relationship with the Holy Spirit. He gives us strength, power and endurance.

Acts 1:8 (NIV)

But you will receive power when the Holy Spirit comes on you.

The Holy Spirit is our source and strength. Without His help we become weak and revert back to thinking like the world. When the Holy Spirit is absent from our daily lives we can begin to live and act like those who are in the flesh.

Galatians 5:16-17 (NLT)

So I say, let the Holy Spirit guide your lives. Then you won't be doing what your sinful nature craves. The sinful nature wants to do evil, which is just the opposite of what the Spirit wants. And the Spirit gives us desires that are the opposite of what the sinful nature desires. These two forces are constantly fighting each other, so you are not free to carry out your good intentions.

The story is told of a Native American man speaking to his grandson:

The boy was only eleven years old at the time and was struggling with his attitude and behaviour. He asked his grandfather, "How do you stop doing the things that are wrong?"

His grandfather replied, "My son, there are two wolves in you; one who wants to do good and the other who only desires that which is bad."

The boy exclaimed, "Yes! How do I stop the bad wolf?"

The old man smiled, knelt down next to the young boy and said, "You simply feed the good wolf!"

The Holy Spirit gives us the strength to do all that God calls us to do.

> **John 6:63 (NLT)**
>
> The Spirit alone gives eternal life. Human effort accomplishes nothing. And the very words I have spoken to you are spirit and life.

My Prayer

Father, I ask that you will strengthen me by your Holy Spirit. Help me to be strong in times of weakness. Help me to walk in faith and integrity. Keep me in your ways; let me know your thoughts and your Word.

I surrender all my hopes, plans, dreams and anxious moments to you. This is the day that you have made, and I know by faith you have created in this day great things for me. I embrace all you have for me. I am more than a conqueror in you.

I am blessed and rich in faith because of what you have done on the cross. Amen!

God-Thoughts & Holy Spirit Promptings

_____

_____

_____

_____

_____

_____

_____

_____

_____

_____

_____

_____

(Chapter 2)
No Entry

Proverbs 4:23 (NLT)

Guard your heart above all else, for it determines the course of your life.

The enemy knows that if he can let us hold anything ungodly in our hearts it will lead to our demise. Most people think, "I do my duty: I go to church, I pray, I worship and I give money. I must be okay!" But the Lord looks beyond what we do to the issues of the heart. The heart of man is, above all else, wicked. David's prayer in Psalm 51 was "Create in me a clean heart, oh Lord." We must guard against lies, cheats, gossip, slander, bitterness, offences and the like. Why? Because they ruin our hearts!

Hebrews 12:15b (NLT)

Watch out that no poisonous root of bitterness grows up to trouble you, corrupting many.

In the natural, a bad heart leads to death; in the spiritual it is the same! Whatever gets lodged in your heart can lead to your spiritual death. Offences are one of the things that cause people to die spiritually. There will always be an opportunity to be offended; however, offence is a choice. Choose not to be offended! As believers, we are to be dispensers of forgiveness.

Mark 11:25 (NIV)

And when you stand praying, if you hold anything against anyone, forgive him, so that your Father in heaven may forgive you your sins.

Forgiveness is in the very nature of God. When we, as His children, practice un-forgiveness we are going against the very nature of God and what He freely gives out to all. A life of un-forgiveness and bitterness will not be a blessed life. There are many people lying in hospital and many others with long-term sicknesses as a direct result of bitterness.

Job 21:25 (NIV)

Another man dies in bitterness of soul, never having enjoyed anything good.

Eight truths about bitterness:

1. Bitterness is the opposite of forgiveness.
2. Bitterness quenches the spirit of God in you.
3. Bitterness is the offspring of un-forgiveness.
4. Bitterness will steal your joy.
5. Bitterness will strangle your life.
6. Bitterness will divert you from your destiny in God.
7. Bitterness will rob you of health and blessings.
8. Bitterness will isolate you from your family and friends.

When you go before God, ask Him to show you your heart and test its motives, and, through the power of the Holy Spirit, He will show you the condition of your heart.

Hebrews 10:22 (NIV)

Let us draw near to God with a sincere heart in full assurance of faith, having our hearts sprinkled to cleanse us from a guilty conscience and having our bodies washed with pure water.

My Prayer

Father, you know me. You know my thoughts and my innermost secrets. You know my strengths and my weaknesses, yet you still call me. Father, I know that I need more of you in my life and I surrender all my ways to you. I give it all up to you and ask that you begin and continue this great work in me.

I know that my thoughts and actions will determine the quality of the believer's life that I experience. I give it all to you. Create in me a clean heart, oh Lord. Amen!

God-Thoughts & Holy Spirit Promptings

_____

_____

_____

_____

_____

_____

_____

_____

_____

_____

_____

_____

(Chapter 3)
Cheap Knock-Off

1 Corinthians 13:13 (NLT)

Three things will last forever—faith, hope, and love—and the greatest of these is love.

When you read the context of this chapter, most of the power gifts are mentioned (faith, speaking in tongues, prophecy and so on), but here Paul is trying to show the reader that most of these things are only partial or for a while, but that the three greatest things are faith, hope and love. Faith means reaffirming and encouraging people in the world. The world today needs faith, it needs God and it needs a hero - Jesus Christ represents all of those and more!

As we belong to Christ we put our hope in him. This starts from a young age and solidifies as we grow. This is why imparting spiritual guidance while kids are young is very important. David puts it this way:

Psalm 71:5 (NLT)

O Lord, you alone are my hope. I've trusted you, O LORD, from childhood.

After hope, Paul then talks about love. Love cannot come from an unclean source, only from a pure heart. Love is us giving up what we want for what God wants for us, because we love Him and we trust Him. That love is reflected every day by how we live our lives.

Listen to this story:

Lucia was a bright-eyed, pretty five-year-old girl. One day when she and her mother were checking out at the supermarket, Lucia saw a plastic pearl necklace priced at £2.00. How she wanted that necklace! When she asked her mother if she would buy it for her, her mother said, "Well, it is a pretty necklace, but it costs an awful lot of money. I'll tell you what. I'll buy you the necklace, and when we get home we can make up a list of chores that you can do to pay for it. And don't forget that for your birthday Grandma just might give you a pound, too. Okay?"

Lucia agreed, and her mother bought the pearl necklace for her.

Lucia worked on her chores very hard every day, and sure enough, her grandma gave her a brand new pound coin for her birthday. Soon, Lucia had paid off the pearls. How Lucia loved those pearls. She wore them everywhere; to school, to bed and when she went out with her mother to run errands.

The only time she didn't wear them was in the shower. Her mother had told her that they would turn her neck green!

Now Lucia had a very loving father. Every night when she went to bed, he would get up from his favourite chair and read Lucia her favourite story.

One night when he finished the story, he said, "Lucia, do you love me?"

An Extra Shot

"Oh yes, Daddy, you know I love you," Lucia said.

"Well, then, give me your pearls."

"Oh! Daddy, not my pearls!" Lucia said. "But you can have Rosy, my favourite doll. Remember her? You gave her to me last year for my birthday. And you can have her tea party outfit, too. Okay?"

"Oh no, darling, that's okay." Her father brushed her cheek with a kiss. "Good night, little one."

A week later, her father once again asked Lucia after her story, "Do you love me?"

"Oh yes, Daddy, you know I love you."

"Well, then, give me your pearls."

"Oh, Daddy, not my pearls! But you can have Ribbons, my toy horse. Do you remember her? She's my favourite. Her hair is so soft, and you can play with it and braid it and everything. You can have Ribbons if you want her, Daddy," Lucia said to her father.

"No, that's okay," her father said and brushed her cheek again with a kiss. God bless you, little one. Sweet dreams."

Several days later, when Lucia's father came in to read her a story, Lucia was sitting on her bed and her lip was trembling. "Here, Daddy," she said, and held out her hand. She opened it and her beloved pearl necklace was inside. She let it slip into her father's hand.

With one hand her father held the plastic pearls and with the other he pulled out of his pocket a blue velvet box. Inside the box were real, genuine, beautiful pearls. He had had them all along. He was waiting for Lucia to give up the cheap stuff so he could give her the real thing.

When we hold on selfishly to things in our lives, we are robbing God of the opportunity to give us the real blessings. Nothing will ever stop God from loving us; no matter what you have done and how disappointed you think God may feel, the fact of the matter is that He loves you and nothing will change that!

Romans 8:34-40 (NLT)

Who then will condemn us? No one—for Christ Jesus died for us and was raised to life for us, and he is sitting in the place of honour at God's right hand, pleading for us.

Can anything ever separate us from Christ's love? Does it mean he no longer loves us if we have trouble or calamity, or are persecuted, or hungry, or destitute, or in danger, or threatened with death? (As the Scriptures say, "For your sake we are killed every day; we are being slaughtered like sheep.") No, despite all these things, overwhelming victory is ours through Christ, who loved us.

And I am convinced that nothing can ever separate us from God's love. Neither death nor life, neither angels nor demons, neither our fears for today nor our worries about tomorrow—not even the powers of hell can separate us from God's love. No power in the sky above or in the earth below—indeed, nothing in all creation will ever be able to separate us from the love of God that is revealed in Christ Jesus our Lord.

My Prayer

Father, I come before you and ask that you will help me to remember your love for me. I align myself to your Word and your Church. As I spread the message of faith and hope let this be wrapped in your unconditional love. Help me to deliver the message of the cross, not only by what I say today, but by how I live my life every day. I reject all the cheap, counterfeit things of this world for your genuine, authentic love. Amen!

God-Thoughts & Holy Spirit Promptings

_____

_____

_____

_____

_____

_____

_____

_____

_____

_____

_____

_____

An Extra Shot

(Chapter 4)

You've Passed

Deuteronomy 8:2 (NKJV)

And you shall remember that the LORD your God led you all the
way these forty years in the wilderness, to humble you and test you,
to know what was in your heart, whether you would keep His
commandments or not.

Testing something shows its quality. When a product is tested, it's
pushed to the limit in order to see what will happen, thus
showing what's called its 'integrity'. God will sometimes allow times
of trial and testing to come our way in order to show us what we are
really like and how much we need Him. Abraham was tested in
Genesis 22: "Take your son, your only son whom you love and
sacrifice him." Step forward the test! Abraham, as you know, passed
the test on all counts because he did not withhold his son. God
provided an offering for Abraham. End of story. Or is it?

Genesis 22:12 (NLT)

"Don't lay a hand on the boy!" the angel said. "Do not hurt him in
any way, for now I know that you truly fear God. You have not
withheld from me even your son, your only son."

We will all face different trials and tests in life. During these storms, if you ask God, He will give you the wisdom and the know-how to get through it. Some trials have to run their course so at the end of the day we can learn how to stand strong.

James 1:2-8 (MSG)

Consider it a sheer gift, friends, when tests and challenges come at you from all sides. You know that under pressure, your faith-life is forced into the open and shows its true colours. So don't try to get out of anything prematurely. Let it do its work so you become mature and well-developed, not deficient in any way. If you don't know what you're doing, pray to the Father. He loves to help. You'll get his help, and won't be condescended to when you ask for it. Ask boldly, believingly, without a second thought. People who "worry their prayers" are like wind-whipped waves. Don't think you're going to get anything from the Master that way, adrift at sea, keeping all your options open.

On the other hand, some trials and tests are of our own making, due to our own poor choices and a lack of obedience to God and His Word. When we choose to get involved in ungodly relationships or live in sinful behaviour then we are simply living in the fruit of disobedience. When we disobey our parents or disregard our leader's words to us then the consequences aren't a test, just bad fruit.

What to do during a season of testing:

1. Meditate on His Word.
2. Draw close to Him.
3. Be in Church.
4. Be faithful.
5. Confess God's Word.
6. Hold on to His promises.
7. Love His presence.
8. Worship Him.

9. Give tithes and offerings.
10. Seek and follow Godly wisdom.

> ### Galatians 6:7 (NIV)
>
> Do not be deceived: God cannot be mocked. A man reaps what he sows.

My Prayer

Father, I come before you and ask that you will search me and reveal what's in my heart. Help me to remove all that does not belong to you and uncover your plan for me during this time. Help me to overcome the temptations and trials of this world as I totally surrender myself to you and your Church. Holy Spirit, be my guide and comforter in the storm. Amen!

God-Thoughts & Holy Spirit Promptings

_____

_____

_____

_____

_____

_____

_____

_____

_____

_____

_____

(Chapter 5)

And You Are?

Jeremiah 1:5-10 (NLT)

"I knew you before I formed you in your mother's womb. Before you were born I set you apart and appointed you as my prophet to the nations." "O Sovereign Lord," I said, "I can't speak for you! I'm too young!" The Lord replied, "Don't say, 'I'm too young,' for you must go wherever I send you and say whatever I tell you. And don't be afraid of the people, for I will be with you and will protect you. I, the Lord, have spoken!" Then the Lord reached out and touched my mouth and said, "Look, I have put my words in your mouth! Today I appoint you to stand up against nations and kingdoms. Some you must uproot and tear down, destroy and overthrow. Others you must build up and plant."

It's amazing to think that someone as important and amazing as God knows you, and knows you by name! My family and I were privileged to visit some very famous cricketers from the West Indies Cricket team. After the match we met up with the players and the assistant coach, David Williams, for a chat and to spend some time together. As we entered the place where the players were there was a lot of security and they didn't have a clue who we were! As we were walking towards the team, security men got up and started moving towards us, looking very concerned. At that moment my friend, David, saw us and shouted "Pastor Chip!" The security men left us and went on their way. Why did they leave us alone? Because the man in charge knew us by name. So it is with God; He knows us and this brings down everything that is set to oppose us!

Colossians 2:13-15 (NLT)

You were dead because of your sins and because your sinful nature was not yet cut away. Then God made you alive with Christ, for he forgave all our sins. He cancelled the record of the charges against us and took it away by nailing it to the cross. In this way, he disarmed the spiritual rulers and authorities. He shamed them publicly by his victory over them on the cross.

Here are some amazing thoughts:

- God knows you.
- He knows everything about you.
- He knows your faults and weaknesses.
- Before you speak, He knows the words you are about to say.
- He calls you and uses you to do great exploits.

Psalm 139:23 (NIV)

Search me, O God, and know my heart; test me and know my anxious thoughts.

No one knows you like you! When we search ourselves the danger is that we focus on the incomplete areas of our lives. We can dwell on the parts that we feel weak in, on the things that we cannot do and on our failures. When God looks at us He sees us as perfect! We still make mistakes and we are still sinful, but He is our Heavenly Father and He loves us very much. Don't look at yourself through your own eyes; see yourself as God sees you. Here are some pitfalls to be mindful of:

- Comparing yourself to others.
- Feeling 'unworthy'.
- Thinking 'My past is too messed up'.
- Thinking 'My future will never be good'.
- Vain imagination.

Matthew 7:11 (MSG)

"Don't bargain with God. Be direct. Ask for what you need. This isn't a cat-and-mouse, hide-and-seek game we're in. If your child asks for bread, do you trick him with sawdust? If he asks for fish, do you scare him with a live snake on his plate? As bad as you are, you wouldn't think of such a thing. You're at least decent to your own children. So don't you think the God who conceived you in love will be even better?"

My Prayer

Father, create in me a clean heart and renew a right spirit in me. Help me to focus on you, for your strength is limitless and your grace is amazing. I ask that today I walk with the steps of faith, with purpose in every stride and with this goal in mind. Help me to be a strong finisher.

Help me, Holy Spirit, to rule over my emotions and thought-life. Let me not remain the same but let me be changed from glory to glory. You are awesome, oh God, and I know that even before I was conceived you already set me aside to do great and effective things for you.

This day I will lift my head up high, and walk with renewed purpose and understanding. Thank you so much, Father, for looking after my every step. Amen!

God-Thoughts & Holy Spirit Promptings

_____

_____

_____

_____

_____

_____

_____

_____

_____

_____

_____

_____

_____

An Extra Shot

(Chapter 6)
Knocking On Heaven's Door

Matthew 6:6 (NLT)

But when you pray, go away by yourself, shut the door behind you, and pray to your Father in private. Then your Father, who sees everything, will reward you.

Praying to God is one of the most useful things you can do. It's a spiritual act that brings physical rewards. Most people are passionate about things that have no benefit to them whatsoever, but prayer benefits the believer in many ways. Here are just a few examples.

When we pray:

1. God listens.
2. God intervenes.
3. Doors are opened.
4. Negative doors are shut.
5. The sick are healed.
6. Miracles take place.
7. Faith grows.

8. God moves.
9. We grow.
10. Delayed answers come our way.

> **Proverbs 15:29 (NLT)**
>
> The LORD is far from the wicked, but he hears the prayers of the righteous.

Those are just a few things to show you what prayer can do. Now, I know you would love these things to happen to you, but do you spend time in prayer for them? When we don't pray, here's what happens:

1. God seems far away.
2. No access to supernatural power, resulting in a life of stress and emotional pain.
3. Blocked access to God-ordained opened doors.
4. Negative things are always around.
5. Sickness comes.
6. No experience of miracles.
7. Faith dies back.
8. God cannot move.
9. We shrink spiritually.
10. Our lives can be characterised by delay, disappointment and discouragement.

I don't know what drives you, what motivates you or where you are in your relationship with the Lord, but a life with God coupled with prayer is dynamic! Most people would love to have the lifestyle of the rich and famous - to have the house, the car, the private villa, to be in the media, to have the best health care, etc. - but prayer places us in the path of God's favour and bountiful blessings.

Solomon communed with God. God appeared to him in a dream and connected with him in a real, tangible way. The result of this was that Solomon's heartfelt prayer was answered, and he was granted the blessings and lifestyle that every king would want as well! It pays to knock on Heaven's door in prayer!

1 Kings 3:10-14 (NLT)

The Lord was pleased that Solomon had asked for wisdom. So God replied, "Because you have asked for wisdom in governing my people with justice and have not asked for a long life or wealth or the death of your enemies—I will give you what you asked for! I will give you a wise and understanding heart such as no one else has had or ever will have! And I will also give you what you did not ask for—riches and fame! No other king in all the world will be compared to you for the rest of your life! And if you follow me and obey my decrees and my commands as your father, David, did, I will give you a long life."

My Prayer

Heavenly Father, I come before you and ask that you will give me grace and mercy. I will lock myself in your presence and daily connect with you. Father, as I do this, help me to grow in you and your Word. Help me to be a person of faith, a person that has wisdom to make the right choices in life. I will give to you of my wealth and my time as I help build your Church. May your Kingdom come and your will be done. I give you all the praise and all the glory. Amen!

God-Thoughts & Holy Spirit Promptings

_____

_____

_____

_____

_____

_____

_____

_____

_____

_____

_____

_____

An Extra Shot

(Chapter 7)
Sin Equals Death

Romans 6:1-4 (MSG)

So what do we do? Keep on sinning so God can keep on forgiving?
I should hope not! If we've left the country where sin is sovereign,
how can we still live in our old house there? Or didn't you realize
we packed up and left there for good? That is what happened in
baptism. When we went under the water, we left the old country of
sin behind; when we came up out of the water, we entered into the
new country of grace—a new life in a new land!

That's what baptism into the life of Jesus means. When we are
lowered into the water, it is like the burial of Jesus; when we are
raised up out of the water, it is like the resurrection of Jesus. Each
of us is raised into a light-filled world by our Father so that we can
see where we're going in our new grace-sovereign country.

Our world and everything in it screams, 'It doesn't matter what
you do once your heart is right!' Well, that's wrong, it does
matter. It's very possible to be both sincere and sincerely wrong! The
wages of sin are still death. Sinful living cannot be part of the
believer's life. You cannot call yourself a believer in Christ and still
wilfully sin. You must turn your back on that lifestyle. Sin may be an

old fashioned, unpopular word but it still brings dreadful consequences.

Galatians 5:16-26 (MSG)

My counsel is this: Live freely, animated and motivated by God's Spirit. Then you won't feed the compulsions of selfishness. For there is a root of sinful self-interest in us that is at odds with a free spirit, just as the free spirit is incompatible with selfishness. These two ways of life are antithetical, so that you cannot live at times one way and at times another way according to how you feel on any given day. Why don't you choose to be led by the Spirit and so escape the erratic compulsions of a law-dominated existence?

It is obvious what kind of life develops out of trying to get your own way all the time: repetitive, loveless, cheap sex; a stinking accumulation of mental and emotional garbage; frenzied and joyless grabs for happiness; trinket gods; magic-show religion; paranoid loneliness; cutthroat competition; all-consuming-yet-never-satisfied wants; a brutal temper; an impotence to love or be loved; divided homes and divided lives; small-minded and lopsided pursuits; the vicious habit of depersonalizing everyone into a rival; uncontrolled and uncontrollable addictions; ugly parodies of community. I could go on.

This isn't the first time I have warned you, you know. If you use your freedom this way, you will not inherit God's kingdom.

But what happens when we live God's way? He brings gifts into our lives, much the same way that fruit appears in an orchard—things like affection for others, exuberance about life, serenity. We develop a willingness to stick with things, a sense of compassion in the heart, and a conviction that a basic holiness permeates things and people. We find ourselves involved in loyal commitments, not needing to force our way in life, able to marshal and direct our energies wisely.

Legalism is helpless in bringing this about; it only gets in the way. Among those who belong to Christ, everything connected with getting our own way and mindlessly responding to what everyone else calls necessities is killed off for good—crucified.

An Extra Shot

Since this is the kind of life we have chosen, the life of the Spirit, let us make sure that we do not just hold it as an idea in our heads or a sentiment in our hearts, but work out its implications in every detail of our lives. That means we will not compare ourselves with each other as if one of us were better and another worse. We have far more interesting things to do with our lives. Each of us is an original.

I've met people who think they are believers in God but continue to lie, cheat, steal, have sex outside of marriage, commit adultery and so on, thinking, 'I can always repent later and God will forgive me.' Don't be fooled; God knows our hearts and sees our motives. We must be holy and live a holy life before our God (1 Peter 1:15-17).

The Bible is filled with warnings regarding those who wilfully sin and the consequence of that lifestyle. I want to encourage you all, 'put off' sin and 'put on' Christ! In other words, you have to do it - it's a conscious act of the will.

Turn away from sin and turn to God. Draw near to Him and He will draw near to you.

2 Samuel 22:26 (NLT)

"To the faithful you show yourself faithful; to those with integrity you show integrity."

My Prayer

Lord Jesus, I come before you and ask you to forgive me of all the things I have done that bring shame and dishonour to you. Father, I ask that you forgive me for those things and help me, through your Holy Spirit, to run away from sin. I ask that, by grace, you cover me, guide me and protect me. I give my heart to you and all that I am belongs to you. You deserve the best and I give the best of my life to you.

Thank you for all you do and thank you for the Church. Help me, Lord, to be holy through what you have done on the cross. Amen!

God-Thoughts & Holy Spirit Promptings

_____

_____

_____

_____

_____

_____

_____

_____

_____

_____

_____

_____

God-Thoughts & Holy Spirit Promptings

_____

_____

_____

_____

_____

_____

_____

_____

_____

_____

_____

_____

(Chapter 8)
We're It

2 Chronicles 7:14 (NLT)

Then if my people who are called by my name will humble themselves and pray and seek my face and turn from their wicked ways, I will hear from heaven and will forgive their sins and restore their land.

What a great scripture on how prayer actually works! We are all called to a deeper level of intimate, passionate prayer; the kind of prayer that gets God's attention. As I read this short passage, eight things occurred to me:

1. We are His people (we belong to Him).
2. Humility precedes genuine, heartfelt prayer.
3. Lack of a prayer life is a sign of living in pride.
4. We are to seek God and not material things.
5. Before God answers any prayer we need to change our lifestyles.
6. God hears our prayers.
7. His first response is to deal with sin, not just give us what we are asking for.
8. For our world/nation to do better, it's down to us!

When you read the scripture with this sort of understanding you soon realise that our world needs us as much as we need God. We are the ones who are called to stand in the gap; we are the ones to pray for the people in the world and we are the ones to plead for their souls!

Have you ever thought that maybe God put you in that school, workplace, or college to make a difference and share His Word?

Jonah 4:10-11 (NLT)

Then the LORD said, "You feel sorry about the plant, though you did nothing to put it there. It came quickly and died quickly. But Nineveh has more than 120,000 people living in spiritual darkness, not to mention all the animals. Shouldn't I feel sorry for such a great city?"

Do you ever feel sorry for the people in your city, town or region? Sorry enough to pray for them and ask God to save them? Or are you so caught up in your world - what you need and what you want - that others come second to you and yours? We are called to prefer others, love our cities and reach our countries for God. When we do this, we soon realise that God works out our problems as we do what He asks us to do.

Philippians 2:3-11 (NLT)

Don't be selfish; don't try to impress others. Be humble, thinking of others as better than yourselves. Don't look out only for your own interests, but take an interest in others, too. You must have the same attitude that Christ Jesus had. Though he was God, he did not think of equality with God as something to cling to.

Instead, he gave up his divine privileges; he took the humble position of a slave and was born as a human being. When he appeared in human form, he humbled himself in obedience to God and died a criminal's death on a cross. Therefore, God elevated him to the place of highest honour and gave him the name above all other names, that at the name of Jesus every knee should bow, in

> heaven and on earth and under the earth, and every tongue confess
> that Jesus Christ is Lord, to the glory of God the Father.

My Prayer

Heavenly Father, I come before you and ask for grace and mercy to be poured out on my city and nation. I thank you for this great land I live in and pray that you will indeed heal it and bless it. Thank you for my great city. I know you are God and I ask, in the name of Jesus, that you do a great work in this city. I bless your name and give you the glory. Amen!

God-Thoughts & Holy Spirit Promptings

(Chapter 9)

My Face In His Book

Matthew 11:28-30 (NLT)

Then Jesus said, "Come to me, all of you who are weary and carry heavy burdens, and I will give you rest. Take my yoke upon you. Let me teach you, because I am humble and gentle at heart, and you will find rest for your souls. For my yoke is easy to bear, and the burden I give you is light."

P art of the Kingdom of God that is often neglected by believers is rest. Not *sleep* but *rest;* leaving all the cares, worries and uncertainties of the future for a life of rest in God. In musical terms a rest is a pause in a piece of music. In the same way, God wants us to pause in life and rest in Him. Wow! God wants us to have a great life by resting in Him. Hebrews talks about 'the promised place of rest' - this is not in Heaven but on Earth. We should have a restful spirit and soul, in life and in His Kingdom. We are not called to be stressed, we are not called to be highly strung, and we are certainly not called to scrape through life! We are called to enjoy life!

John 10:10 (NLT)

The thief's purpose is to steal and kill and destroy. *My purpose is to give them a rich and satisfying life.*

This rest comes from the Word of God. It's more than reading the Word, it's more than knowing the Word, it's applying it! The greatest, most restful thing a person can do is to read the Word of God. You won't find rest by reading magazines or romance novels (and certainly not by living on social networking sites), only by hiding your face in His book!

Hosea 4:6 (NIV)

My people are destroyed from lack of knowledge. "Because you have rejected knowledge, I also reject you as my priests; because you have ignored the law of your God, I also will ignore your children."

A weak, stressful and emotion-ruled life is one that is in need of a one-to-one with God. A life that is not habitually in prayer, reading the Word and in Church will be an unstable one. When we ignore these pivotal things we literally destroy our lives. A stressed, un-rested life is a symptom of a person who is not hiding in God and His Word.

Isaiah 40:31 (NLT)

But those who trust in the Lord will find new strength. They will soar high on wings like eagles. They will run and not grow weary. They will walk and not faint.

My Prayer

Father, I want to have rest in you. I don't want the burdens of this life; I want to rest in you. I want your yoke and your burdens. I refuse to be brought down by the cares of this world and the uncertainty of tomorrow. I put myself under your yoke.

Father, I confess areas in my life where I have no rest and hand them all over to you. I will not be busy with the things that pull me down, but busy in you! I give my talent, my time, my touch and my treasure to you, for your burden is easy and your yoke is light. Amen!

God-Thoughts & Holy Spirit Promptings

_____

_____

_____

_____

_____

_____

_____

_____

_____

_____

_____

_____

(Chapter 10)
All You Need Is Love

Isaiah 9:6-7 (NLT)

For a child is born to us, a son is given to us. The government will
rest on his shoulders. And he will be called: Wonderful Counsellor,
Mighty God, Everlasting Father, Prince of Peace. His government
and its peace will never end. He will rule with fairness and justice
from the throne of his ancestor David for all eternity. The
passionate commitment of the LORD of Heaven's Armies will make
this happen!

Mary didn't have an ultrasound scan, a midwife or the comfort
of a hospital with her family all around her. She was in a barn,
surrounded by animals (ladies - there was no 'gas-and-air' either!).
Mary gave birth to God's Son, Jesus. He came into the world as
Saviour and King. She was not surprised that the baby was a boy; it
just confirmed the things the angels spoke to her.

Matthew 1:20-21 (NLT)

As he considered this, an angel of the Lord appeared to him in a
dream. "Joseph, son of David," the angel said, "do not be afraid to
take Mary as your wife. For the child within her was conceived by

the Holy Spirit. And she will have a son, and you are to name him Jesus, for he will save his people from their sins."

This kind act of God - sending His only Son - was motivated by love and nothing else! John 3:16 tells us that 'God so loved the world that He sent His only Son'. Love was the motivating factor for Christ being born into the world. God loves you! His love for you reaches high and wide. Paul, the writer of Romans, puts it this way:

Romans 8:37-39 (NLT)

No, despite all these things, overwhelming victory is ours through Christ, who loved us. And I am convinced that nothing can ever separate us from God's love. Neither death nor life, neither angels nor demons, neither our fears for today nor our worries about tomorrow—not even the powers of hell can separate us from God's love. No power in the sky above or in the earth below—indeed, nothing in all creation will ever be able to separate us from the love of God that is revealed in Christ Jesus our Lord.

Can you imagine that God loves us? He not only created us but He also loves us. Love is a strong emotion. Love brings hope, strength, courage, faith, blessing and sacrifice. Love can cause a person to do 'supernatural' things. No matter how amazing it feels to be the object of human love, nothing compares to the love that God has towards us. His love is desperately needed by the world.

'Being unwanted, unloved, uncared for, forgotten by everybody, I think that is a much greater hunger, a much greater poverty than the person who has nothing to eat. Do not think that love, in order to be genuine, has to be extraordinary. What we need is to love without getting tired.' - **Mother Teresa**

But this love is linked to obedience. If we truly love God then we will obey His Word. You cannot truly love God and knowingly disobey His Word.

John 14:23 (NLT)

Jesus replied, "All who love me will do what I say. My Father will love them, and we will come and make our home with each of them."

My Prayer

Father, I come before you as your child and ask for grace and mercy for the times I am selfish. I love you, Lord. Thank you for your Word and your thoughts towards me. I choose to obey your Word; I choose to trust you and I choose to put you first. Guide me by your Holy Spirit. Amen!

God-Thoughts & Holy Spirit Promptings

_____

_____

_____

_____

_____

_____

_____

_____

_____

_____

_____

_____

An Extra Shot

Chapter 11

He Makes Me Strong

2 Samuel 22:3 (NKJV)

The God of my strength, in whom I will trust; My shield and the horn of my salvation, My stronghold and my refuge; My Saviour, You save me from violence.

When you are young, it's easy to think that the superheroes you read about are real. It's a nice feeling to know that, in this world of comics and fairy tales, there's a hero just around the corner to help you if you're in need. But have you ever noticed that all these heroes have a weakness? No matter how great they are, Superman, Spiderman and every other has a weakness or is susceptible to failure.

Not so with our God! He is our strength, He is mighty, and He can tell no lie. The devil cannot stop Him and the world cannot break Him - He is our God! Just one word from God created the world and just one word brought His only Son as the real saviour of mankind. He died and rose again, bringing life and freedom forevermore. In Christ there are no limits to what He can and will do, in and through you. Even when you feel unable, through Him you can say 'Yes, I can!'

Luke 5:5 (MSG)

Simon said, "Master, we've been fishing hard all night and haven't caught even a minnow. But if you say so, I'll let out the nets." It was no sooner said than done—a huge haul of fish, straining the nets past capacity. They waved to their partners in the other boat to come help them. They filled both boats, nearly swamping them with the catch.

This world of no limits can only happen in God and will usually require a big step of faith. When we 'let go and let God', all things become possible. When we hold onto God, God holds on to us. When God says 'Let go!' He has already ordered another great plan to come into effect. This strength is called faith and only comes when we, His children, trust in Him.

There are times in life when you will not understand what is going on. In these moments, things may seem to have spiralled out of control and all your best-laid plans seem like a joke. This is when trust in God makes you strong. It becomes like the sun to Superman - it strengthens you to embrace the invisible and do the impossible.

Psalm 22:4-5 (NIV)

In you our fathers put their trust; they trusted and you delivered them. They cried to you and were saved; in you they trusted and were not disappointed.

My Prayer

Father, thank you for life in you! I embrace all the good things you have for me, and I stand strong on your Word. I gather my thoughts and hopes and fix them on you. I will come to your house with praise on my lips and a new song in my heart. I take confidence in knowing that no weapon that forms against me shall ever prosper. I am blessed to be a blessing. Bless your Holy name! Amen!

God-Thoughts & Holy Spirit Promptings

_____

_____

_____

_____

_____

_____

_____

_____

_____

_____

_____

_____

God-Thoughts & Holy Spirit Promptings

_____

_____

_____

_____

_____

_____

_____

_____

_____

_____

_____

_____

An Extra Shot

Chapter 12

Yes Man

2 Corinthians 1:20 (NIV)

For no matter how many promises God has made, they are "Yes" in Christ. And so through him the "Amen" is spoken by us to the glory of God.

The 'Yes' attitude to God always brings rewards - from Abraham to David and from Daniel to Paul; these were people who lived saying 'Yes' to God and His Word. It's easy to say 'Yes', however it's more than just what you say that counts, it's how you live your life. You may say 'Yes' with your lips but actually be saying 'No' in your life by the choices you make and the way you live.

A person who lives a lifestyle of 'Yes' to God always receives great blessings. 'Yes' to God means 'Yes' to Church and 'Yes' to Church means 'Yes' to His chosen leadership. The promises of God are tied into your willingness to serve under the pastors and leaders God has placed over your life. Accountability not only provides a safety net but also releases favour.

Psalm 90:17 (NIV)

May the favour of the Lord our God rest upon us; establish the work of our hands for us— yes, establish the work of our hands.

God will establish His work, however this 'Yes' depends on us doing our part to live in the reality of God's promises. 'Yes' calls for action.

Saying 'Yes' means:

1. We give our four T's (time, talent, treasure and touch).
2. We commit to His house (not choosing to miss Church).
3. We obey His Word.
4. We love each other.
5. We obey our leaders.

And the list goes on! You see, living a lifestyle of 'Yes' manifests in the same way as trust; it's seen more than heard. So, are you a 'Yes' man or woman in God? Before you answer, remember: it's not what you say but how you live that matters!

The word 'Yes' is also synonymous with loyalty. I see them as interwoven in attitude and behaviour. When a person is loyal to another, the 'Yes' attitude is shown in their trust and love. It has nothing to do with sinful intentions and all to do with giving God the glory. In others words, 'Yes' means 'Yes' and 'No' means 'No'!

Matthew 5:37 (NIV)

Simply let your 'Yes' be 'Yes,' and your 'No', 'No'; anything beyond this comes from the evil one.

My Prayer

Gracious Father, I thank you for life in you. I bring my all to you, I will not hold back in my words and thoughts to you, as you have never held back from me. I thank you that through Jesus Christ I have access and can live in the 'yes' attitude. I commit my all to you. Thank you, Father. Amen!

God-Thoughts & Holy Spirit Promptings

_____

_____

_____

_____

_____

_____

_____

_____

_____

_____

_____

_____

An Extra Shot

Chapter 13

What's On Your Mind?

Isaiah 55:8-11 (NLT)

"My thoughts are nothing like your thoughts," says the LORD. "And my ways are far beyond anything you could imagine. For just as the heavens are higher than the earth, so my ways are higher than your ways and my thoughts higher than your thoughts. The rain and snow come down from the heavens and stay on the ground to water the earth. They cause the grain to grow, producing seed for the farmer and bread for the hungry. It is the same with my word. I send it out, and it always produces fruit, it will accomplish all I want it to, and it will prosper everywhere I send it."

Recently, my wife, kids and I went down to South Wales for a short break. On the way back the heavens opened and it began to snow! We were driving through a mini blizzard! Driving when it's snowing is amazing as you see the millions and millions of snowflakes hitting the windscreen. Suddenly the above scripture from Isaiah 55 popped into my mind. God's thoughts are likened to those snowflakes falling - millions and millions of them - and every one of His thoughts toward you and me is good! He has only great thoughts and great plans for us.

Jeremiah 29:11 (NLT)

For I know the plans I have for you," says the LORD. "They are plans for good and not for disaster, to give you a future and a hope.

God, our loving Father, showers down these amazing thoughts that soon become words which, with time and commitment to His Church, bring prosperity in our lives. Prosperity is not just about money but about a great and peace-filled journey through life.

The enemy has plans for our lives as well. His plans are to 'steal, kill and destroy'. Jesus' plans are the exact opposite; to give you life and bring rich satisfaction! As you go about your day, if you see snow or rain think about this: every drop that hits you is like a God-thought falling on you - and they are only filled with goodness! Remember His thoughts about you.

Psalm 139:17-18 (NLT)

How precious are your thoughts about me, O God. They cannot be numbered! I can't even count them; they outnumber the grains of sand! And when I wake up, you are still with me!

My Prayer

Heavenly Father, I thank you for today, this wonderful day that you have made. I choose to rejoice and be glad! I know that you only have good thoughts towards me and an awesome future in store for me. I surrender all my hopes and dreams, fears and anxious moments to you. Father, I remember the awesome promises that await those who love and trust in you. Thank you so much for your many blessings on me. Amen!

An Extra Shot

God-Thoughts & Holy Spirit Promptings

_____

_____

_____

_____

_____

_____

_____

_____

_____

_____

_____

_____

God-Thoughts & Holy Spirit Promptings

_____

_____

_____

_____

_____

_____

_____

_____

_____

_____

_____

_____

An Extra Shot

Chapter 14

Who's In Charge?

> **Matthew 6:24 (NLT)**
>
> "No one can serve two masters. For you will hate one and love the other; you will be devoted to one and despise the other. You cannot serve both God and money."

Jesus talks about money more than any other single topic in the Bible. Yes, money! James tells us that the love of money is the root of all evil. Now, money itself is not bad; it's the 'love' of money (being ruled by needing or making money over needing God) that is bad. How do we curb that love of money? Simple - by giving it away! Yes, give it away! The scriptures tell us a lot about helping the poor, supporting the needy and building His Church by giving our money.

> **Deuteronomy 15:10 (NLT)**
>
> Give generously to the poor, not grudgingly, for the LORD your God will bless you in everything you do.

As we have seen in the news, when there is a natural disaster the world's first response is to donate money to the cause. Why?

Scripture tells us in Ecclesiastes 10:19; "A feast is made for laughter, and wine makes life merry, but money is the answer for everything."

This scripture is obviously not talking about money bringing long-term happiness, fulfilment or salvation, but about it being the solution in times of need. It is also teaching us how to avoid the sin of covetousness. Money can invoke different reactions in people; some just love to give and others only take. As believers - God's representatives on Earth - we need to reflect Him not only in the way we speak but also in how we handle money.

When you bring your tithes, offerings and First Fruits, it's a way of saying, "It's not my money and I will not be ruled by it. I will not let money tell me what to do and how I should live my life. I live by the Word of the Lord and I depend on Him for life. I will not be mastered by money, I will master it!"

So, who is your master? You alone know the answer.

2 Corinthians 9:9-11 (NLT)

As the Scriptures say,

"They share freely and give generously to the poor. Their good deeds will be remembered forever."

For God is the one who provides seed for the farmer and then bread to eat. In the same way, he will provide and increase your resources and then produce a great harvest of generosity in you.

Yes, you will be enriched in every way so that you can always be generous. And when we take your gifts to those who need them, they will thank God.

My Prayer

Father, I come before you and I lay my heart open. I ask that your Holy Spirit speaks to me and shows me if I am ruled by money. As I go to your house I prepare myself to give my tithes and First Fruits offering with joy to you. I will not be ruled by my emotions when it comes to money, but I will be ruled by your Word.

I will not let fear of the future lead me, I will trust in you. I know that your Word is a lamp to my feet, a light to the path of life. I surrender my mind, will and emotions to your Word. In the mighty name of Jesus. Amen!

God-Thoughts & Holy Spirit Promptings

_____

_____

_____

_____

_____

_____

_____

_____

_____

_____

_____

_____

(Chapter 15)

Let's Dance

Psalm 30:11 (NLT)

You have turned my mourning into joyful dancing. You have taken away my clothes of mourning and clothed me with joy.

' **G**iving may hurt but what you get causes shouts of joy' (Psalm 126, author's version). The human tendency is not to give but to keep for ourselves. We see it as our right to hold on to what we have, simply because it belongs to us. When God asks us to give He is hitting at the heart of what really matters most to mankind: "I work hard for what I get, why should I give it away?" There is only one condition to giving and that's obedience. No matter how deeply you search through the Bible, there's only one thing God blesses us for and that's obedience to His Word.

Matthew 6:31-32 (NLT)

"So don't worry about these things, saying, 'What will we eat? What will we drink? What will we wear?' These things dominate the thoughts of unbelievers, but your heavenly Father already knows all your needs."

He knows what you need and He also knows what surprises are awaiting you. In the midst of something bad, He has already begun to work out something good. That's what faith is; trusting in God despite what you see around you. I trust God so I bring to Him my tithe and my offerings. I don't hold back because of what I see, I trust Him all the way.

Psalm 28:7 (NLT)

The LORD is my strength and shield. I trust him with all my heart. He helps me, and my heart is filled with joy. I burst out in songs of thanksgiving.

Have you ever seen someone on a bus or train with headphones on listening to music? They sing along, tap their feet and even do the occasional jig. To you or anyone else watching it seems ridiculous, but if you were to put on the headphones the chances are you would sing and dance too! It's the same with trusting God. People around you are in their own turmoil with their own problems and struggles, but you have blocked yourself out of it by tuning into God through the Holy Spirit. Your ear is tuned to His voice and you are dancing to a different tune!

1 Corinthians 14:7-8 (NLT)

Even lifeless instruments like the flute or the harp must play the notes clearly, or no one will recognize the melody. And if the bugler doesn't sound a clear call, how will the soldiers know they are being called to battle?

My Prayer

Lord Jesus, I bring all my worries and anxious moments before you. I trust in you. You know my needs and I believe that you have already made a way for me. I will not let worry or fear dominate my mind. I give all my cares to you and rejoice in you! Thank you for the greatest blessing of all, this great salvation. Amen!

God-Thoughts & Holy Spirit Promptings

_____

_____

_____

_____

_____

_____

_____

_____

_____

_____

_____

_____

(Chapter 16)
"Don't Worry, Just Trust Me!"

> **Psalm 25:2 (NIV)**
>
> In you I trust, O my God. Do not let me be put to shame, nor let my
> enemies triumph over me.

Trust is seen and not just heard. Lots of people say, 'Yes, I trust God!', but it's more than what you say - it's what you do that counts. Our actions speak louder than words in the ears of God. We grow in our trust in God when we let go and let God take control. God deserves our highest praise, but that praise is only valid with the seal of trust on it. God will never let you down; He is faithful, He is loving and He is God, however, God only works when we move out in faith and obey Him at His every word.

> **Psalm 9:10 (NIV)**
>
> Those who know your name will trust in you, for you, LORD, have
> never forsaken those who seek you.

When you trust someone or something, you have total, one hundred percent confidence that no matter what people's opinions are, every little thing is going to be alright. Holding on to God means that regardless of what's happening around me, I know that He holds my future in His arms. Isn't it funny how we can trust in things very easily but with God we question Him? We trust in our cars to take us where we are going and keep us safe; we trust in planes; we trust that when we sit on a chair it will hold us. Every day we practise these small trust-steps with things all around us, yet with God we find it challenging to trust in Him.

> **Psalm 20:7 (NIV)**
>
> Some trust in chariots and some in horses, but we trust in the name of the LORD our God.

With this is mind, I bring my tithe and my offerings to Him as I trust Him; I am committed to His house above my own; I continue in fellowship with His people and I grow in my trust in Him. In return I can be trusted by Him with my time, talent, treasure and touch. You see, when we talk about trusting God we are talking about us actually making a conscious effort to change and adjust things in our lives.

God is unchanging; He doesn't need to change as He is perfect in every way. The very character and nature of God makes me confident that I can trust in Him.

Here are some things to consider:

1. His supremacy: God is the Supreme Being. He is not merely a different type of being or a superior being but the Supreme Being.
2. His uniqueness: God is unique. The Bible describes Him in Greek as *monogenesis*, (one of a kind, having a unique nature).
3. He is eternal: He has always existed and will always exist. He had no beginning and will never cease to exist.
4. His omniscience: He knows all things.
5. His omnipotence: He is all-powerful.
6. His omnipresence: He is everywhere at the same time.

An Extra Shot

7. He is self-existent: God is the only thing that had no beginning and that was not created by something else.
8. He is holy: Holy means pure, undefiled.
9. He exists in a triune nature: the one God is a single trinity consisting of three distinct persons (Father, Son and Holy Spirit).

My Prayer

My loving Father, I come before you and I throw all my silly thoughts and helpless moments into your arms. I know you are my Father, who only wants good things for me. This weekend I will prepare myself for your house and come ready to show my trust in you by putting you first in everything I do and with all that I have. I love you, Father. Amen!

God-Thoughts & Holy Spirit Promptings

_____

_____

_____

_____

_____

_____

_____

_____

_____

_____

_____

_____

(Chapter 17)
Seek Him, Not Blessings

Deuteronomy 10:20 (NLT)

You must fear the LORD your God and worship him and cling to him.

No one likes a person who uses another just to get something they want. Sometimes people can do things in God's Kingdom looking for rewards or money in return. This is not always a bad thing; however, serving and obedience should be driven by love and not rewards. God loved us so much that He sent His only Son. This gift was driven totally by love.

John 3:14-18 (NLT)

And as Moses lifted up the bronze snake on a pole in the wilderness, so the Son of Man must be lifted up, so that everyone who believes in him will have eternal life. For God loved the world so much that he gave his one and only Son, so that everyone who believes in him will not perish but have eternal life. God sent his Son into the world not to judge the world, but to save the world through him. There is no judgment against anyone who believes in

him. But anyone who does not believe in him has already been
judged for not believing in God's one and only Son."

If we truly love the Lord we will truly worship Him. Worship is not
based on feelings or rewards, but on obedience. We were created to
worship God. Without true worship and adoration of God we lose our
true sense of purpose. When a man takes his eyes off of God then he
begins to worship himself and what he created with his own hands. It
could be a job, a house, a relationship or even a ministry that comes
before the Lord.

Exodus 32:2-4 (NLT)

So Aaron said, "Take the gold rings from the ears of your wives
and sons and daughters, and bring them to me." All the people took
the gold rings from their ears and brought them to Aaron. Then
Aaron took the gold, melted it down, and moulded it into the shape
of a calf. When the people saw it, they exclaimed, "O Israel, these
are the gods who brought you out of the land of Egypt!"

It's so easy to forget that it is the Lord who has blessed us and that
nothing we do deserves His blessing. When we take our eyes off the
Lord and worship other things, they begin to take God's place in our
lives. It seems today that a lot of churches and Christians only talk
about blessings. Now, God truly wants to bless His people, but I often
wonder if we are truly seeking Him or just seeking blessings. They
can be very different things. If God chooses not to bless us, will we
still worship Him? What if seeking Him costs you your very life?

Daniel 3:16-18 (NLT)

Shadrach, Meshach, and Abednego replied, "O Nebuchadnezzar,
we do not need to defend ourselves before you. If we are thrown
into the blazing furnace, the God whom we serve is able to save us.
He will rescue us from your power, Your Majesty. But even if he
doesn't, we want to make it clear to you, Your Majesty, that we
will never serve your gods or worship the gold statue you have set
up."

My Prayer

Father, I come into your presence and want to say sorry if I am seeking blessings above you. From this day on I will seek you with all of my heart, mind and soul. I am not motivated to seek you for what you can do for me, but simply because of what you have already done. I love you, Lord, and will worship your holy name. Amen!

God-Thoughts & Holy Spirit Promptings

_____

_____

_____

_____

_____

_____

_____

_____

_____

_____

_____

_____

_____

An Extra Shot

(Chapter 18)
Stick 'em Up

Leviticus 18:4 (NIV)

You must obey my laws and be careful to follow my decrees. I am
the LORD your God.

Many years ago, while my wife and I were living in Portland,
USA, I remember seeing a bumper sticker that said, "Relax,
God is my co-pilot." It didn't take long for someone to come up with
the response, "If God is your co-pilot, then you need to swap seats!"

Obedience is about surrender, that bumper sticker illustrates this.
Many Christians are happy with God being their second-in-command,
but for our lives to take a full turn for the better God must be the
commander-in-chief. When we let Him take control, His blessings
and all His good things are ours for keeps!

Leviticus 25:18 (NIV)

Follow my decrees and be careful to obey my laws, and you will
live safely in the land.

Disobedience equals pain; my boys know this lesson well! When we disobey the law of our houses, of the land, or of the Lord, our portion will be pain and tears. When we live a life of obedience, blessings will overtake us. Sin has a way of delaying us and, if we don't root it out, it will destroy us! If you ever use a satnav you can see what I mean. If you take a wrong turn the satnav will say 'recalculating', which now means it's going to take longer to get where you are going!

We live in a generation that thinks, "Oh, well. I messed up, but God will forgive me." And we think that everything will be okay! God can forgive our sins but we will reap the fruit of that disobedience. There are consequences for every bad choice. We see this in the life of Esau. His actions cost him his inheritance. We can sometimes sell ourselves short and miss out on God's best in our lives for the shallow pleasures of sin. This is what Paul had to say about Esau:

> **Hebrews 12:15-17 (NIV)**
>
> See to it that no one misses the grace of God and that no bitter root grows up to cause trouble and defile many. See that no one is sexually immoral, or is godless like Esau, who for a single meal sold his inheritance rights as the oldest son. Afterward, as you know, when he wanted to inherit this blessing, he was rejected. He could bring about no change of mind, though he sought the blessing with tears.

A life of obedience is a life that is surrendered! Have you ever seen the old Western movies when the marshal comes into the saloon, kicks open the doors, draws his guns and says, "Stick 'em up!"? Everyone - without question - puts their hands up, because if they didn't the consequence would be death. So it is with a life of surrender. When we fail to surrender to God, sin takes over our lives. The Bible tells us that the wages of sin is death. Jesus came that we all might have a rich and satisfying life. The choice is yours.

John 10:10 (NLT)

The thief's purpose is to steal and kill and destroy. My purpose is to give them a rich and satisfying life.

My Prayer

Jesus, I truly surrender all to you. I am sorry for the times I gave you the backseat in my life. Today, I give you the first place. Holy Spirit, try me and test me to see if there are any sinful ways in me. I totally surrender to your Word, your Church and your will in my life. Thank you, Lord, for this amazing grace being shown to me. Amen!

God-Thoughts & Holy Spirit Promptings

_____

_____

_____

_____

_____

_____

_____

_____

_____

_____

_____

_____

Chapter 19

Think Twice Before You Speak

Matthew 12:35-37 (NLT)

"A good person produces good things from the treasury of a good heart, and an evil person produces evil things from the treasury of an evil heart. And I tell you this, you must give an account on judgment day for every idle word you speak. The words you say will either acquit you or condemn you."

'Measure twice and cut once' were the wise words of my woodwork teacher in high school. In other words, double-check your measurements and get it right the first time because mistakes can be costly! These wise words from my teacher may be stressing the importance of double-checking measurements, but they also apply equally to speaking! Imagine, for a moment, your words are being recorded daily and then played back in front of the world. I wonder; if we were in that situation, what would our words bring back to us? What would people think about you?

The scriptures tell us that death and life are in the tongue. The Psalmist put it this way:

Psalm 34:13 (NLT)

Then keep your tongue from speaking evil and your lips from telling lies!

Lies have a funny way of coming back to haunt you. Lies should never be part of the vocabulary of God's people. Lying undermines the very heart of God's Word. Jesus came as the way, the truth and the life. Lying is one of the things that the Lord absolutely hates!

Proverbs 6:16-18 (NLT)

There are six things the LORD hates—no, seven things he detests: haughty eyes, a lying tongue, hands that kill the innocent, a heart that plots evil, feet that race to do wrong.

When we tell lies or speak evil of others our words are being recorded, not by the media, but by the Lord Himself. These words can either bring you freedom or cause condemnation. The words you speak have power in them; speak them to edify each other and glorify God. One of my sayings is: "Words are like wild horses; once they are free you can never get them back!" Your words are a gift; use them to be kind and gentle. Speak in all honesty and integrity and don't tell half-truths (which are really lies). For example, if you're tired, don't say you're ill - just be honest and tell the truth. It's better to be embarrassed today and live in freedom tomorrow - humble pie is best eaten warm! Use your words wisely!

Proverbs 13:2-4 (NLT)

Wise words will win you a good meal, but treacherous people have an appetite for violence. Those that control their tongue will have a long life; opening your mouth can ruin everything.

My Prayer

Father, help me today, by your Holy Spirit, to guard my tongue. Help me to only speak words that have life and healing in them. Father, I repent for the times when my words were used to cut down, to destroy, or to lie. I ask for forgiveness, Lord. Help me to have a revelation of how powerful my words are. Amen!

God-Thoughts & Holy Spirit Promptings

_____

_____

_____

_____

_____

_____

_____

_____

_____

_____

_____

_____

(Chapter 20)

Get Your Prayer On

Philippians 4:5-7 (NKJV)

Let your gentleness be known to all men. The Lord is at hand. Be anxious for nothing, but in everything by prayer and supplication, with thanksgiving, let your requests be made known to God; and the peace of God, which surpasses all understanding, will guard your hearts and minds through Christ Jesus.

Most of us struggle to bridge the gap between what we know and what we do. The things we know that we should do, we don't and the things we know that we shouldn't do, we do! It's time to lead from your heart and not from your emotions. Many feelings can float around in our minds on any given day, but what makes us victorious is our ability to remain constant and levelheaded when things are potentially chaotic or even just mundane. This ability is not natural but supernatural in design and only possible through the Holy Spirit. The Holy Spirit is our comforter, strength and the one who convicts. He guides us where we should go and gently encourages us about what we should do.

John 16:13 (CEV)

The Spirit shows what is true and will come and guide you into the full truth. The Spirit doesn't speak on his own. He will tell you only what he has heard from me, and he will let you know what is going to happen.

Prayer is something we all need to do more of. You don't need to pray loud, boisterous, eloquent prayers - or even so-called 'powerful prayers' - you are already praying to a powerful God! Prayers need not last hours either. They can be for just a few minutes every day, when you call out to God in that moment of need, or when you are feeling low, or when the promises that you are waiting for seem to be fading away.

You build up your faith by reading the Word and praying. When we do this we see that 'yet in all these things, we are more than conquerors!' Why? Prayer gets us to depend on God rather than on working things out in our own minds.

Psalm 4:1 (NKJV)

Hear me when I call, O God of my righteousness! You have relieved me in my distress; Have mercy on me, and hear my prayer.

Prayer guided by the Holy Spirit is even more effective. There are moments in our lives when God, through His Holy Spirit, may bring someone to mind and cause us to stop what we're doing and pray intently for them. This is not the only time we should pray though, we should always be praying, no-matter what!

If there was ever anyone you could think of who wouldn't need to pray, it would have been Jesus. Yet the Bible tells us that Jesus, before He faced the day, before He healed the sick and before He spoke the Word, got up early and prayed!

The best way to start every day is in prayer. Yes, it may cost you some sleep - getting up 15 minutes before normal or even early in the morning - to call on God, but these are the times that we prepare for the unseen, hidden challenges of life. I often think that if we could match the time we spend worrying (or even sleeping) with time in prayer, how much more effective, and even more enjoyable, our lives would be.

Mark 1:35-39 (NKJV)

Now in the morning, having risen a long while before daylight, He went out and departed to a solitary place; and there He prayed. And Simon and those who were with Him searched for Him. When they found Him, they said to Him, "Everyone is looking for You." But He said to them, "Let us go into the next towns that I may preach there also, because for this purpose I have come forth." And He was preaching in their synagogues throughout all Galilee, and casting out demons.

My Prayer

Father, I commit not only to your Church but to your Word, and I commit to be a praying believer. I am sorry for the times I have spent not praying about things and just worrying or complaining. Help me, Lord, though the Holy Spirit, to be a person who prays. I will rise early and seek you, oh Lord. Amen!

God-Thoughts & Holy Spirit Promptings

_____

_____

_____

_____

_____

_____

_____

_____

_____

_____

_____

_____

(Chapter 21)

Man In The Mirror

Matthew 18:3 (NIV)

And he said: "I tell you the truth, unless you change and become like little children, you will never enter the kingdom of heaven."

There are things about ourselves we all need to change - bad habits, personal hang-ups and more! Some people try to change their appearance by spending thousands of pounds on plastic surgery to look a certain way, thinking that it will make them feel much better than they do now. Others change their job or the country they live in, and some even change their husband or wife, looking for improvement and a better quality of life. But the change we need to make is not on the outside or related to other people, it's within ourselves. The biggest room in our lives is the room for improvement! We can all improve when it comes to getting where God wants us to be. Perhaps we need to change from worrying about tomorrow to being warriors in Christ. This may mean having faith over how you feel on any given day.

Judges 6:12 (NIV)

When the angel of the LORD appeared to Gideon, he said, "The LORD is with you, mighty warrior."

When God calls us, He is not looking necessarily at what is to hand, but at what we can be through Him. So we must then deny ourselves, pick up our cross and follow Him. This requires change! To deny yourself means you put your feelings and emotions aside and you do what Christ's Word tells you to do. In some circumstances we stop and wait, in others we go. How do we know what to do at any given point? Well, we listen to His Word and heed direction from our leaders.

Hebrews 13:17 (NIV)

Obey your leaders and submit to their authority. They keep watch over you as men who must give an account. Obey them so that their work will be a joy, not a burden, for that would be of no advantage to you.

This takes a level of childlike faith; we trust that in all things God is working for good. We listen to our leaders over our friends and even what some family members may say. Why? Because God's Word asks us to! Any decision that takes you out of Church is a bad decision. You cannot always find another church; you should be where the Lord has placed you and planted you.

These principles require us to have childlike faith, but don't mistake *childlike* for *childish* - they are two very different things! Take these words and practice them in your everyday life. Remember, your spiritual growth is seen in what you do with your free time!

Philippians 4:4-8 (NIV)

Rejoice in the Lord always. I will say it again: Rejoice! Let your gentleness be evident to all. The Lord is near. Do not be anxious about anything, but in everything, by prayer and petition, with thanksgiving, present your requests to God. And the peace of God, which transcends all understanding, will guard your hearts and your minds in Christ Jesus. Finally, brothers, whatever is true, whatever is noble, whatever is right, whatever is pure, whatever is lovely, whatever is admirable—if anything is excellent or praiseworthy—think about such things.

My Prayer

Father, I ask that through your Holy Spirit you show me the areas where I need to change. Help me to remember your Word and apply it with childlike faith in my life. I surrender my mind, my will and my emotions to you. I ask you, Lord, to do your work in me. I give you all the glory. Amen!

God-Thoughts & Holy Spirit Promptings

_____

_____

_____

_____

_____

_____

_____

_____

_____

_____

_____

(Chapter 22)

Are You All Packed?

2 Peter 3:10 (NLT)

But the day of the Lord will come as unexpectedly as a thief. Then the heavens will pass away with a terrible noise, and the very elements themselves will disappear in fire, and the earth and everything on it will be found to deserve judgment.

I love going on holiday with my family, but the part that brings the least joy is packing! Packing is preparation for the journey ahead. You pack what you need according to where you are going. Some people over-pack and some don't pack enough. Any journey calls for preparation ahead of time.

In this Christian life we need to remember that we are only visitors on Earth and that our real home is with the Lord, so we live our lives as heavenly citizens and not earthly ones.

Philippians 3:20 (NIV)

But our citizenship is in heaven. And we eagerly await a Saviour from there, the Lord Jesus Christ.

This means we are ready always to be with our Lord. This doesn't call for some weird doctrine that expects people to be constantly gazing upwards as at any minute the Lord will return! It calls for our lives to be lived with purpose and in the realisation that whatever we are going through on this Earth is only for a moment. Paul puts it this way:

2 Corinthians 4:16-18 (NLT)

That is why we never give up. Though our bodies are dying, our spirits are being renewed every day. For our present troubles are small and won't last very long. Yet they produce for us a glory that vastly outweighs them and will last forever! So we don't look at the troubles we can see now; rather, we fix our gaze on things that cannot be seen. For the things we see now will soon be gone, but the things we cannot see will last forever.

Carrying lots of baggage on a journey can be very stressful, and many believers today have too much baggage! We limp and stumble through life, not enjoying our Christian walk, as we carry needless things that Jesus took away on the Cross. We need to cast all our cares and burdens on the Lord. Jesus said this:

Matthew 11:30 (NLT)

"For my yoke is easy to bear, and the burden I give you is light."

Don't over-pack for this journey; take off some of those heavy weights and just enjoy being saved, knowing that soon you will be ready to be with the Lord. Praise is a good way to shed baggage, just fall in love with Jesus all over again and soak in His presence!

Psalm 51:7-15 (MSG)

Soak me in your laundry and I'll come out clean, scrub me and I'll have a snow-white life. Tune me in to foot-tapping songs, set these once-broken bones to dancing. Don't look too close for blemishes, give me a clean bill of health. God, make a fresh start in me, shape

> a Genesis week from the chaos of my life. Don't throw me out with the trash, or fail to breathe holiness in me. Bring me back from gray exile, put a fresh wind in my sails! Give me a job teaching rebels your ways so the lost can find their way home. Commute my death sentence, God, my salvation God, and I'll sing anthems to your life-giving ways. Unbutton my lips, dear God; I'll let loose with your praise.

My Prayer

Father, I ask that, through your Holy Spirit, you show me any areas in my life where I am carrying excess baggage. Lord, help me to remove these burdens from my life and give me strength to overcome. Amen!

God-Thoughts & Holy Spirit Promptings

(Chapter 23)

Be Real

2 Peter 1:3-9 (NLT)

By his divine power, God has given us everything we need for
living a godly life. We have received all of this by coming to know
him, the one who called us to himself by means of his marvellous
glory and excellence. And because of his glory and excellence, he
has given us great and precious promises. These are the promises
that enable you to share his divine nature and escape the world's
corruption caused by human desires. In view of all this, make every
effort to respond to God's promises. Supplement your faith with a
generous provision of moral excellence, and moral excellence with
knowledge, and knowledge with self-control, and self-control with
patient endurance, and patient endurance with godliness, and
godliness with brotherly affection, and brotherly affection with love
for everyone. The more you grow like this, the more productive and
useful you will be in your knowledge of our Lord Jesus Christ. But
those who fail to develop in this way are short-sighted or blind,
forgetting that they have been cleansed from their old sins.

These days, we are flooded with so many fake things. People are
happy to have items of clothing, movies and CDs (to name only
a few) that are cheap, pirated versions of the real thing. Companies

spend billions of pounds trying to keep their products from being ripped off, copied and pirated. The Christian life can become a cheap, pirated version of the real thing too. We can live double lives; who we are in public is different to who we are behind closed doors. Peter is encouraging us here that we need to be real and live godly lives, and he is showing us that we have already been given everything we need to live this life through the knowledge of God. This knowledge is more than intellectual perception; it's a real, felt, walked relationship with Him. It's not about perfection but obedience and us adding to our faith.

Now, when it comes to us being forgiven our sin, it is not about human effort, for it was all taken away on the cross! We don't need humanistic psychology or Christian counselling, we need to leave it at the cross. When we try to live the Christian life by adding worldly principles we are being nearsighted and foolish. Paul says this:

Galatians 3:1-3 (CEV)

You stupid Galatians! I told you exactly how Jesus Christ was nailed to a cross. Has someone now put an evil spell on you? I want to know only one thing. How were you given God's Spirit? Was it by obeying the Law of Moses or by hearing about Christ and having faith in him? How can you be so stupid? Do you think that by yourself you can complete what God's Spirit started in you?

We cannot add anything to salvation, however we *can* add to our faith. Peter encourages us to add these things:

1. Goodness (valour and excellence).
2. Knowledge (personal time with Him, knowledge of Him and His ways).
3. Self-control (restrain ungodly impulses).
4. Endurance (press in/on, not lapsing, staying power).
5. Godliness (holiness, righteousness, honesty, not cheating).
6. Love.

We cannot live an effective Christian life by trying to apply the knowledge of the world instead of the knowledge of God. Not only do we know Him, but He knows all our thoughts, our weaknesses and our ways! David puts it this way:

Psalm 139:1-7 (NLT)

O LORD, you have examined my heart and know everything about me. You know when I sit down or stand up. You know my thoughts even when I'm far away. You see me when I travel and when I rest at home. You know everything I do. You know what I am going to say even before I say it, LORD. You go before me and follow me. You place your hand of blessing on my head. Such knowledge is too wonderful for me, too great for me to understand! I can never escape from your Spirit! I can never get away from your presence!

Wow! God knows all this and He still chooses us and calls us by name! He has forgiven us of all our sins and set us free!

John 8:36 (Amp)

So if the Son liberates you [makes you free men and women], then you are really and unquestionably free. Don't be caught up in digging up past sins, enjoy the believer's life as it was all paid for on the cross, be real!

My Prayer

Lord, I align my thoughts and desires with your thoughts and desires. I ask that everything I do genuinely reflects you in all your ways. I will not cheapen my salvation by living a double-standard life. I will honour you in all I do. Help me, by your Holy Spirit, to live on the path of righteousness before you. Amen!

God-Thoughts & Holy Spirit Promptings

_____

_____

_____

_____

_____

_____

_____

_____

_____

_____

_____

(Chapter 24)
Come On, You Can Do It

Hebrews 10:35-37 (NKJV)

Therefore do not cast away your confidence, which has great reward. For you have need of endurance, so that after you have done the will of God, you may receive the promise: "For yet a little while, And He who is coming will come and will not tarry."

The difference between victory and failure is endurance. Jesus knew how important endurance was; the Bible tells us in Hebrews:

Hebrews 12:2 (NIV)

'Let us fix our eyes on Jesus, the author and perfector of our faith, who for the joy set before him *endured the cross*, scorning its shame, and sat down at the right hand of the throne of God.'

Jesus 'endured' the cross. He pushed against His natural urge to quit because He saw you and me. If I have to be somewhere to do something, no matter whether I enjoy it or not, I will do everything I can to be there. There are two things I really dislike: people who do not fulfil their promises and people who give weak excuses. No one likes a quitter and I have a saying at home: 'No wimps!'

I find that most people will ultimately do what they really want to, but very few will push themselves in God through the Church. Some will let tiredness, the weather or some other excuse keep them from accessing all they have in God. As my spiritual father, Colin Cooper, says: 'A man will do what he wants to do.'

Jesus was no quitter! He never gave up or gave in; He fought to the very end. Many people say 'Yes' to God - as far as wanting His best, living in His favour and experiencing all the good things He has in store - but very few will give that higher level of commitment to Him through His Church. The author of Hebrews gave this warning:

Hebrews 10:25 (NLT)

And let us not neglect our meeting together, as some people do, but encourage one another, especially now that the day of his return is drawing near.

We all live busy lives and we all have moments when life itself brings challenges, but we are to remain focused by being in Church. Encourage each other to get to the house of the Lord; you should never miss church by choice!

I remember once, when I was in Kenya a few years back, I met a lady who, for me, showed what endurance really means. I was leading some meetings in a church and I found out that this woman had walked for two days with her very small child to get to the meetings because her child was sick and she believed that by being there he would be healed. You know what, that child was healed! She had to camp overnight at the side of the road (which was not safe due to criminals and other dangers) but she remained focused that God would heal her child and change her situation - and she received what she believed for!

The Bible is full of great men and women who endured to the end; they never gave up and never surrendered. Let me ask you a few questions: Are you a quitter? Are you in need of some endurance? What things keep you from the house of the Lord?

What you do as far as Church and God are concerned will determine what you receive. Dreams without discipline are only a fantasy. Endure to the end!

Matthew 24 makes eye-opening reading for the believer. Jesus tells us about the future and what things will be like. Here is just a short excerpt:

Matthew 24:9-14 (NLT)

"Then you will be arrested, persecuted, and killed. You will be hated all over the world because you are my followers. And many will turn away from me and betray and hate each other. And many false prophets will appear and will deceive many people. Sin will be rampant everywhere, and the love of many will grow cold. But the one who endures to the end will be saved. And the Good News about the Kingdom will be preached throughout the whole world, so that all nations will hear it; and then the end will come."

My Prayer

Father, I repent for the times that I gave up without really pressing in. I ask for your grace for the times that I made poor excuses for not being in your house. Today I have decided to endure, to overcome and to go on strong, no matter what. I commit fully to your house and your Word; I will give my all as you give me your all. Amen!

God-Thoughts & Holy Spirit Promptings

_____

_____

_____

_____

_____

_____

_____

_____

_____

_____

_____

(Chapter 25)
How Deep Is Your Love?

John 14:23-24 (MSG)

"Because a loveless world," said Jesus, "is a sightless world. If anyone loves me, he will carefully keep my word and my Father will love him—we'll move right into the neighbourhood! Not loving me means not keeping my words. The message you are hearing isn't mine. It's the message of the Father who sent me."

In 1977, The Bee Gees released the song *How Deep is Your Love?* It became a huge hit and even today is still sung by many. The song was about searching for something real within a relationship that two people can share. Although secular in its approach, the message is nonetheless still relevant: how deep is your love for Him?

A love for Jesus is not only shown by what we say, but by how much we obey His words through the instrument of the local Church. This message of love was not just sent to you and me but to the whole world, and through the Church we are all to proclaim this unconditional love that He has shown to us.

Romans 8:38-39 (NLT)

And I am convinced that nothing can ever separate us from God's love. Neither death nor life, neither angels nor demons, neither our fears for today nor our worries about tomorrow—not even the powers of hell can separate us from God's love. No power in the sky above or in the earth below—indeed, nothing in all creation will ever be able to separate us from the love of God that is revealed in Christ Jesus our Lord.

God made a commitment to love us and nothing can ever separate us from Him except wilful sin. How great is our God! Not only does He care for us, He absolutely and unconditionally loves us! However, He expects us to love Him in the same measure. Jesus, chatting with Peter in the gospel of John, asks an intriguing question: 'Do you love me more than these?' (John 21:15). He is asking us the same question today, 'Do you love me more than...?'

The truth is that those who love Him obey Him. Love calls for a level of devotion and loyalty similar to marriage, where two people commit to be with each other, no matter what happens in life. Love often calls for sacrifice; John 3:16 says that, 'God so loved the world that *He gave* His only Son.' Jesus was sacrificed for you and me because of God's love. Love will cost you - it cost God His Son! Loving and giving go hand-in-hand. A love for God will cause you to give the following: your time, your talent, your treasure and your touch. These are not in vain as God is a rewarder!

God is looking for people who will build His Church. His Church becomes more and more effective when we show this unconditional love to each other, not expecting anything in return, just as Jesus did. Show one another how deep His love is in you, both through the Church and in everyday life.

Acts 2:42-46 (NLT) - The Believers Form a Community

All the believers devoted themselves to the apostles' teaching, and to fellowship, and to sharing in meals (including the Lord's Supper), and to prayer. A deep sense of awe came over them all, and the apostles performed many miraculous signs and wonders. And all the believers met together in one place and shared everything they had. They sold their property and possessions and shared the money with those in need. They worshipped together at the Temple each day, met in homes for the Lord's Supper, and shared their meals with great joy and generosity.

Practical ways to show Christ's love:

1. Smile! Just being warm and welcoming goes a long way.
2. Be a giver. Be generous towards each other, help support one another and give to your local Church.
3. Build relationships/friendships with one another. Go beyond your own comfort and boundaries, love one another and include new people in your circle of friends.
4. Commit to His Church. Our love for God is seen in the level of commitment we give to His house. It's the practical way of seeing where you belong and who you are devoted to.
5. Connect with new people. When someone new comes to Church or gives their heart to God we should all help that person to connect with Christ and His Church. This means that as leaders and mature believers we call and connect with them, invite them into our homes and take them out with us. This is being Jesus in the flesh!
6. Be an encourager. Don't be negative in life! Every time you open your mouth, make sure something good and positive comes out of it! Whatever is in your heart will be shown through your lips.
7. Be a listener. Be careful that you are not always talking; make sure you are also listening! Becoming a great listener is a great life skill. Nothing is more frustrating than having someone talk non-stop to you or having someone else answer for you!

8. Do what you promised to do. Nothing weakens other peoples' respect for you more than if you are always forgetting to do what you said you would. It can be as simple as returning a missed phone call or performing a quick task - although they are very small things they show what sort of person you are!

Psalm 48:8-10 (NLT)

We had heard of the city's glory, but now we have seen it ourselves the city of the LORD of Heaven's Armies. It is the city of our God; he will make it safe forever. O God, we meditate on your unfailing love as we worship in your Temple. As your name deserves, O God, you will be praised to the ends of the earth. Your strong right hand is filled with victory.

My Prayer

Father, I love you and give my all to you. Thank you, Lord, for your unfailing love; it endures for a lifetime! I love you and I love your house. Thank you, Lord, for calling me into your Kingdom to be a worker in your house. I show my love for you by my commitment to your house. Amen!

God-Thoughts & Holy Spirit Promptings

_____

_____

_____

_____

_____

_____

_____

_____

_____

_____

_____

_____

God-Thoughts & Holy Spirit Promptings

_____

_____

_____

_____

_____

_____

_____

_____

_____

_____

_____

_____

An Extra Shot

Chapter 26

I Am Legend

1 Peter 2:9 (NLT)

But you are not like that, for you are a chosen people. You are royal priests, a holy nation, God's very own possession. As a result, you can show others the goodness of God, for he called you out of the darkness into his wonderful light.

Man was created to have fellowship. Without intimate fellowship we move from thriving to surviving. In the world today there are many clubs and groups that meet and have their own form of community - golf clubs, fishing groups, biking and bikers groups, (to me, the most peculiar one is the UFO club that travels all over the world to meet up with and talk to others about their experiences!) - because God put in each human being the need for relationship, someone we can share our lives and our achievements with and who can help us in our hour of need. The Church is more than a social club; it is the bride of Christ, the chosen instrument of change on Earth. The Church and Christ are united together as one body; to hurt the Church is to hurt Christ Himself.

Ephesians 5:32 (NLT)

This is a great mystery, but it is an illustration of the way Christ and the church are one.

There is nothing more exciting than Church! The practical working of the Church involves being good, kind and courteous. The Church is not full of perfect people, but people with flaws and weaknesses - we are all imperfect people serving a perfect God. We can, however, be made perfect through Jesus. I have met so many people who have walked out of churches because someone let them down or showed their imperfections. I often say to our church body, 'offence is a choice; choose not to get offended'. Offended people soon become bitter people who are so twisted in their thinking that it can result in sickness. Jesus forgives us of so many trespasses, likewise, we as the Church - the bride of Christ - forgive those who have wronged us and even hurt us. Take to heart the words of Jesus:

John 15:12-14 (MSG)

I've told you these things for a purpose: that my joy might be your joy, and your joy wholly mature. This is my command: Love one another the way I loved you. This is the very best way to love. Put your life on the line for your friends. You are my friends when you do the things I command you. I'm no longer calling you servants because servants don't understand what their master is thinking and planning. No, I've named you friends because I've let you in on everything I've heard from the Father.

Notice the terms of this friendship with Christ hinge on 'when you do the things I command you'. What's the command? 'Love one another the way I loved you.' How did Christ love us? By dying for us while we were still sinners! While we were deserving of death, God sent His only Son for you and me. Now we become the prodigy of Christ. It's easy to love those who love you and those who do things for you, but this calls for loving your enemies and those who do you harm. The perfect love of Christ needs to be shared through His imperfect people, and it's by the grace of God we can do this. When we have compassion for the poor, when we help the sick and needy and when we forgive others in all things, we show people Christ working through us. We are now His legend!

We often fall prey to forgetting what God has done for us and through us, so take a moment to remember these things:

1. Remember Christ being born into this world.
2. Remember the cross.
3. Remember the words of Christ.
4. Remember the joy of salvation.
5. Remember God's gift of the Holy Spirit.
6. Remember the Church.
7. Remember His love.
8. Remember His peace.
9. Remember His blessings.
10. Remember how He forgave you of your sins.

Romans 8:35-39 (CEV)

Can anything separate us from the love of Christ? Can trouble, suffering, and hard times, or hunger and nakedness, or danger and death? It is exactly as the Scriptures say, "For you we face death all day long. We are like sheep on their way to be butchered." In everything we have won more than a victory because of Christ who loves us. I am sure that nothing can separate us from God's love - not life or death, not angels or spirits, not the present or the future, and not powers above or powers below. Nothing in all creation can separate us from God's love for us in Christ Jesus our Lord!

My Prayer

Father, thank you for your Church. Jesus, give me a revelation of your Church. Thank you for life in you. Help me to walk together with you and your people despite potential upsets and conflicts. Father, help me to see the best in others. I want to be a dispenser of grace and forgiveness. Amen!

God-Thoughts & Holy Spirit Promptings

_____

_____

_____

_____

_____

_____

_____

_____

_____

_____

_____

_____

_____

God-Thoughts & Holy Spirit Promptings

_____

_____

_____

_____

_____

_____

_____

_____

_____

_____

_____

_____

(Chapter 27)

In A Galaxy Far, Far Away...

Ephesians 3:9-11 (NLT)

I was chosen to explain to everyone this mysterious plan that God, the Creator of all things, had kept secret from the beginning. God's purpose in all this was to use the church to display his wisdom in its rich variety to all the unseen rulers and authorities in the heavenly places. This was his eternal plan, which he carried out through Christ Jesus our Lord.

Long before the world was ever created, even before time, God planned that the Church would be used to display His wisdom and power. The Church is to be so powerful and dynamic that Jesus said this:

Matthew 16:18 (CEV)

So I will call you Peter, which means "a rock." On this rock I will build my church, and death itself will not have any power over it.

There is such power and force in the Church that even Hell itself cannot withstand it! Even though Adam failed and Israel failed, the Church will never fail nor will it die.

The Church is not about buildings, websites, carpets, chairs or logos; it's about people; people from every walk of life, every tribe and tongue, both young and old. What makes the Church so powerful? Well, it's not the miracles or the spectacular but the people in it, people who work together with one heart and one spirit!

1 Peter 2:9-10 (NKJV)

But you are a chosen generation, a royal priesthood, a holy nation, His own special people, that you may proclaim the praises of Him who called you out of darkness into His marvellous light; who once were not a people but are now the people of God, who had not obtained mercy but now have obtained mercy.

The fact of the matter is that miracles will not change the world and nor will signs and wonders. In fact, the Bible tells us that in the last days many will be deceived by them! Jesus did so many miracles that in the book of John it says that 'if they were all written down, I suppose the whole world could not contain the books that would be written' (John 21: 25). Many people who saw and witnessed the great miracles of Jesus were not changed, so there must be an answer outside of the supernatural. There is, and it's called the Church!

Many believers are looking for power in all the wrong places. They think that something outside the Church will provide the answer, or even that some para-church activity (anything in the name of Christ that takes a person out of the local church) is the key. Some are only concerned about whether their needs are being met. When we have a revelation of the glorious bride of Christ and sow our lives into the Church, we experience what the power of God really is. The Church changes lives; that's a miracle in itself! Today, commit yourself to your church, be a worker in this ministry and give your all for the Church. Why? Because this is what Christ did!

Acts 2:42-47 (NLT) - The Believers Form a Community

All the believers devoted themselves to the apostles' teaching, and to fellowship, and to sharing in meals (including the Lord's Supper), and to prayer. A deep sense of awe came over them all, and the apostles performed many miraculous signs and wonders. And all the believers met together in one place and shared everything they had. They sold their property and possessions and shared the money with those in need. They worshipped together at the Temple each day, met in homes for the Lord's Supper, and shared their meals with great joy and generosity—all the while praising God and enjoying the goodwill of all the people. And each day the Lord added to their fellowship those who were being saved.

Acts 4:32-35 (NLT) - The Believers Share Their Possessions

All the believers were united in heart and mind. And they felt that what they owned was not their own, so they shared everything they had. The apostles testified powerfully to the resurrection of the Lord Jesus, and God's great blessing was upon them all. There were no needy people among them, because those who owned land or houses would sell them and bring the money to the apostles to give to those in need.

My Prayer

Lord, give me a revelation of your Church. I don't want to be swept aside into all the cosmetics of the believer's life so that I miss the most exciting thing on Earth, which is Church. I devote all that I am to all that you are building. Amen!

God-Thoughts & Holy Spirit Promptings

_____

_____

_____

_____

_____

_____

_____

_____

_____

_____

_____

(Chapter 28)
It's Full On

Matthew 16:18 (NLT)

Now I say to you that you are Peter (which means 'rock'), and upon this rock I will build my church, and all the powers of hell will not conquer it.

This is a scripture that makes you shout 'bring it on!' Such power and such authority belong to the believer *only* through the Church. When believers try to demonstrate these powers outside God's chosen instrument, we see a pirated version of God's life-changing strength. This power is not given to a certain race or tribe; being a Christian or an Israelite or some other denomination doesn't give you access - this power is only available through the Church! Every tribe and tongue can enjoy access through the Church.

Acts 1:8 (NKJV)

But you shall receive power when the Holy Spirit has come upon you; and you shall be witnesses to Me in Jerusalem, and in all Judea and Samaria, and to the end of the earth.

We lose access to these powers when we get distracted by what I call 'the cosmetics of the Church.' There are many things that can take our time, so we have to balance them by asking the question 'Does it build Church?' Having been involved with building Church for a long time, I've seen the great results that people who have committed themselves to building Church have achieved. I can say without a doubt that the Church is God's instrument of change on the Earth! Church is good for single people, for marriages, for young people, for mature people, for different races - Church is even good for the economy! Commitment to God is commitment to Church. The way we treat Church is a reflection of the way we treat God.

Acts 9:1-6 (NIV)

Meanwhile, Saul was still breathing out murderous threats against the Lord's disciples. He went to the high priest and asked him for letters to the synagogues in Damascus, so that if he found any there who belonged to the Way, whether men or women, he might take them as prisoners to Jerusalem. As he neared Damascus on his journey, suddenly a light from heaven flashed around him. He fell to the ground and heard a voice say to him, "Saul, Saul, why do you persecute me?" "Who are you, Lord?" Saul asked. "I am Jesus, whom you are persecuting," he replied. "Now get up and go into the city, and you will be told what you must do."

Now, I must balance this with the fact that not all churches function the way they should. However, as these churches begin to understand their call and how leadership should work, then even they can be effective and life changing. Our goal as we build Church is to glorify the Lord by living the believer's life.

Since before He laid the foundations of the Earth, Church has been God's idea! It was hidden in God Himself. Church is not 'Plan B' because Adam sinned or second to the Jews as they rejected Christ; Church is God's instrument on the Earth.

Ephesians 3:8-11 (NLT)

Though I am the least deserving of all God's people, he graciously gave me the privilege of telling the Gentiles about the endless treasures available to them in Christ. I was chosen to explain to everyone this mysterious plan that God, the Creator of all things, had kept secret from the beginning. God's purpose in all this was to use the church to display his wisdom in its rich variety to all the unseen rulers and authorities in the heavenly places. This was his eternal plan, which he carried out through Christ Jesus our Lord.

As we sink our teeth into what God has for us, living life with a purpose and to reach all men, understand that it's through the Church that we pull down the powers of darkness and reveal God's grace and purpose. Yes, it's full on, but we can boldly say to the enemies of God, 'Bring it on; I'm part of the Church!' In summary, this is what we should be doing:

1. Commit to Church. Church is God's plan; to be outside of Church is to be outside of God's plan.
2. Commit to each other. As we are part of Church we are meant to relate and build relationships with each other. Church is not about attending but belonging. My best friends were all found in Church!
3. Commit to the leadership. God appoints a leadership that should govern and lead the Church. The leader's job only becomes effective once people follow! I understand that there are some leaders who have abused their position and authority in the past, however we are told to obey our leaders and to pray for them. Gossip is never mentioned!

Hebrews 13:17 (NIV)

Obey your leaders and submit to their authority. They keep watch over you as men who must give an account. Obey them so that their work will be a joy, not a burden, for that would be of no advantage to you.

My Prayer

Lord, thank you so much for the Church. Without the Church, where would I be? I ask that, through your Holy Spirit, I commit all my ways to your House. Thank you, Father, for this amazing gift that brings so many blessings in my life. Amen!

God-Thoughts & Holy Spirit Promptings

_____

_____

_____

_____

_____

_____

_____

_____

_____

_____

_____

God-Thoughts & Holy Spirit Promptings

_____

_____

_____

_____

_____

_____

_____

_____

_____

_____

_____

_____

(Chapter 29)
Jesus And A Satnav

Proverbs 4:5b (NLT)

"Don't forget my words or turn away from them."

Something that most people are loath to do, and are even afraid of, is change. Change is something we all experience, however the older you get, the more set in your ways you can become. One of the hardest things to do is to get people to change; change their ideas, the way they do things or even their habits. Recently, this was brought home to me as my wife and I decided to get a satnav for our holiday. I found out that there are many different ways to get to a place - and even some which are much quicker than the route we have always taken! But, being uncomfortable with the idea of going a different way, we double-checked the settings on the satnav to see if it was right - we checked it four times! Guess what, it was right, and it got us to our destination quicker, avoiding traffic and without stress! All we had to do was let go and trust that the machine was right. The Bible tells us this when it comes to trusting the Lord:

Proverbs 3:5-6 (NLT)

Trust in the LORD with all your heart; do not depend on your own understanding. Seek his will in all you do, and he will show you which path to take.

When you give your life to Jesus it is great, wonderful and awesome. However, you soon begin to recognise many habits in your life that need to change. Jesus comes as The Way, the one who knows the best way to go and how we should conduct ourselves. He comes and begins to say 'turn left' in a situation where you have always turned right, and total trust causes you to turn left when everything within you wants to go right. This can be in relationships, values, work ethic, trust or even within the realm of your emotions. Emotions can cause you to go back to bad habits and negative responses to life's upsets. Jesus had emotions, but emotions never had Him. The Christian life is about total trust in God and His Word.

2 Samuel 22:31 (NLT)

"God's way is perfect. All the LORD's promises prove true. He is a shield for all who look to him for protection."

When we change our ways for His ways, our life's journey becomes less stressful and more joyful! When we listen to the advice of our pastors, leaders and parents on the issues of life, God begins to work in us and speak to us. Relationships are one of the things that many people can get wrong very easily. Be it with friendships or courtships, within that relationship God begins to speak to you about that person. Maybe it's through your parents, your pastors or your leaders, but you know He is saying 'turn left'. If you don't, it does not mean He doesn't love you anymore, it may just delay your journey. He has to recalculate a new route which will end up taking you longer to get where He wants you to be. Be wise today and listen to His voice. He knows where He is taking you! All other routes carry with them bad consequences. Here are some pointers to help you on this great journey:

1. Read your Bible and pray every day (read through and meditate on Proverbs 3-5).
2. Obey your pastors, parents and Church leaders (Hebrews 13:17; Colossians 3:20).
3. Be in Church (Hebrews 10:24-25).
4. Listen to and obey the Word (Judges 2:17).
5. Worship, no matter how difficult things may be (Joshua 5 and 6).
6. Be faithful (Psalms 31:23).
7. Be loyal with your heart and your finances (2 Kings 20:3; 2 Timothy 1:13).

1 Kings 15:14-15 (NKJV)

But the high places were not removed. Nevertheless Asa's heart was loyal to the LORD all his days. He also brought into the house of the LORD the things which his father had dedicated, and the things which he himself had dedicated: silver and gold and utensils.

My Prayer

Holy Spirit, help me to listen to your voice above all other voices. This day I fine tune my hearing and sharpen my obedience to you and your Word. Holy Spirit, be my guide, my source and my comforter. Fill me afresh, oh Lord, with your Holy Spirit. Amen!

God-Thoughts & Holy Spirit Promptings

_____

_____

_____

_____

_____

_____

_____

_____

_____

_____

_____

An Extra Shot

(Chapter 30)
What Are You Going To Do About It?

John 14:23 (NLT)

Jesus replied, "All who love me will do what I say. My Father will love them, and we will come and make our home with each of them."

We all expect obedience from each other. If we make a request or give a command, we expect others to do it without question. However, most people don't like 'just' obeying. Some seek explanation and clarification, but Jesus is looking for total obedience to His Word. When He asks us to do something, He just wants us to do it!

John 2:5 (CEV)

Mary then said to the servants, "Do whatever Jesus tells you to do."

Mary knew that His request might seem ridiculous or impossible, but all things are possible if you just obey Him - no questions, just obey the command. Obedience to Jesus is not based on our feelings, the economy or even our culture, but on a willing heart. When we obey God's Word, it shows how real our relationship with Him is. It reveals in whom we trust.

> ### Psalm 18:2 (NKJV)
>
> The LORD is my rock and my fortress and my deliverer; My God, my strength, in whom I will trust; My shield and the horn of my salvation, my stronghold.

Trust is a conscious act of surrender, surrendering all that I am for all that He is! This obedience is not limited to Him, but also to His servants and representatives on Earth. We should obey our parents (if you want long life - Ephesians 6:1; Colossians 3:20), we should obey our pastors and leaders (Hebrews 13:17) and also our rulers, government and authorities (Titus 3:1; Romans 13:1). In fact, the Bible tells us in Romans 13 that these people are appointed by God.

Look at what is says in the book of Samuel:

> ### 1 Samuel 15:22 (NLT)
>
> "But Samuel replied, 'What is more pleasing to the LORD: your burnt offerings and sacrifices or your obedience to his voice? Listen! Obedience is better than sacrifice, and submission is better than offering the fat of rams'"

The great servants of God we read about in Hebrews 11 that were hailed and honoured for their great faith were all men and women who obeyed God, demonstrating faith even when faced with fear.

Obedience to God will take three things:

1. Trust.
2. Courage.
3. Faith.

Trust means that you know He will never let you down, no matter what! He will be there for you and He is faithful. Courage is only needed when God asks you to do something that fills you with fear. It could be as simple as sharing a prophetic word or stepping out by faith and purchasing a new home or starting a business. And Faith knows that if God has spoken it, it will come to pass.

You cannot come up with the words you need to hear from God by yourself. Hearing from God gives you a word that enables you to hang on when everything else is crumbling around you (Romans 10:17).

Faith lets you hang on until you've got a word from God, and prayer and fasting enable you to switch off the distractions around you and listen to Him. Some people get into trouble because they go ahead and start a business, buy a home or get into a relationship *hoping* that God approves but without actually *hearing* from Him. Listen for the Word of God, and *when you hear it*, just obey!

So what should I do?

1. Seek God in prayer and fasting.
2. Make big decisions slowly.
3. Seek Godly advice (pastors and leaders).
4. Read the Word (have a daily reading plan).
5. Step out and trust that God will come through.
6. Don't obey God based on money, just obey.
7. Raise up your children and teens in God's way (bring them to Church; Church should be part of life).
8. Keep your eyes on Jesus.

Psalm 119:104-106 (NLT)

Your commandments give me understanding; no wonder I hate every false way of life. Your word is a lamp to guide my feet and a light for my path. I've promised it once, and I'll promise it again. I will obey your righteous regulations.

My Prayer

Father, I will obey you! I will not negotiate with your words or your commands; I will follow them all the days of my life. Many may come against me, but I will stand strong on your Word. I will obey those whom you have put over me as they are in right standing with you. Help me, oh Lord, to trust in your unfailing Word. Amen!

God-Thoughts & Holy Spirit Promptings

_____

_____

_____

_____

_____

_____

_____

_____

_____

_____

_____

_____

God-Thoughts & Holy Spirit Promptings

_____

_____

_____

_____

_____

_____

_____

_____

_____

_____

_____

_____

(Chapter 31)
Living On A Prayer

Luke 11:1 (NLT)

Once Jesus was in a certain place praying. As he finished, one of his disciples came to him and said, "Lord, teach us to pray, just as John taught his disciples"

We all need to pray more. Very few believers would say 'I pray enough.' Prayer is very much needed in our daily lives. Jesus taught His disciples how to pray, showing them a method and outline for prayer. If there was anyone who could do without praying it would have been Jesus (being the Son of God!), however, He prayed. He had a lifestyle of prayer and prayed early in the morning (Mark 1: 35-39). Without prayer we lose the ability to be effective in the Kingdom of God. Without prayer we cannot 'do all things' as it is prayer that enables us to do all that God has for us to do. Prayer is our source of power through the Holy Spirit.

Finding a time to pray can stop you from actually praying! I find early in the morning before the house wakes up a good time to pray. It's important to start your day right and give God first place.

Psalm 5:3 (NIV)

In the morning, O LORD, you hear my voice; in the morning I lay my requests before you and **wait** in expectation.

Psalm 57:8 (NLT)

Wake up, my heart! Wake up, O lyre and harp! I will wake the dawn with my song.

There's something dynamic that happens when believers stand in prayer. Prayer changes things and prayer opens doors; supernaturally, it takes us to another level in our walk with God. It's also important to *wait* on God. Don't try to help God out but actually *wait* in prayer!

Psalm 27:14 (NLT)

Wait patiently for the LORD. Be brave and courageous. Yes, wait patiently for the LORD.

When we pray our faith goes to a whole new level. According to Pastor Dick Iverson, there are four steps to faith:

1. Plant the seed by hearing the Word of God.
2. Understand the promises of God.
3. Believe the promises of God.
4. Act on the Word of God and receive your healing or whatever you asked for!

As you read on in Luke 11, you see that the Lord wants us to pray without giving up. He says in verse 8b: 'if you keep knocking long enough, he will get up and give you whatever you need because of your shameless persistence.' Tie this scripture with Luke 18:1-8 (the Parable of the Persistent Widow) and you see that the Lord is saying keep on praying and the door will be opened; keep on seeking and you will find me; keep on asking and you will receive.

Imagine a page with two columns. At the top of the first column you have the title 'Worry' and the other column is headed 'Prayer'. Now, let me ask you a question: Which one of the columns has more in it? Do you worry more or pray more? How about if you do the same with complaining; do you complain more than you actually pray?

Prayer is the number one remedy for stress and sleepless nights. As you pray you are literally handing over all your worries and cares to Him and you soon begin to find rest, peace and answers in His presence. As the Bible tells us, 'in His presence there is fullness of joy!', so make time to pray!

Psalm 86:5-7 (NKJV)

For You, Lord, are good, and ready to forgive, and abundant in mercy to all those who call upon You. Give ear, O LORD, to my prayer; And attend to the voice of my supplications. In the day of my trouble I will call upon You, For You will answer me.

My Prayer

Oh, Holy Spirit, remind me of what great strength that it is I gain as I pray. Help me to have a regular, daily prayer time with you, oh Lord. I long to spend time with you and listen to your voice. I surrender my business to you and give up my free time to call upon your name. Amen!

God-Thoughts & Holy Spirit Promptings

_____

_____

_____

_____

_____

_____

_____

_____

_____

_____

_____

_____

An Extra Shot

(Chapter 32)
Me? Worry? No!

Matthew 6:25 (NLT)

That is why I tell you not to worry about everyday life—whether you have enough food and drink, or enough clothes to wear. Isn't life more than food, and your body more than clothing?

This is a sobering scripture. When you read the full text, you soon find out that Jesus is saying when you worry you are showing that you have little faith!

Matthew 6:30 (NLT)

And if God cares so wonderfully for wildflowers that are here today and thrown into the fire tomorrow, he will certainly care for you. Why do you have so little faith?

The word 'worry' here literally means 'be anxious for nothing' or 'take no careful steps'. In other words, don't be cautious because your Heavenly Father knows what you need and has already provided the answer. He guides the steps of the righteous.

The answer for worry is faith. Faith comes by hearing, and hearing by the Word of the Lord. Without God's Word in our lives we become harnessed by fear, anxiety and ungodly thoughts. It's so easy to worry, especially when you have information at your fingertips, so you should be careful of unqualified information spoken into your life.

When worry shows its face, let faith arise in you. Faith is the remedy for fear and worry. Here are seven things about worry (taken from my book, *God, a Mocha & Me*):

1. Worry is a sin.
2. Worry is a thief.
3. Worry magnifies lies.
4. Worry distorts facts and truths.
5. Worry will stop you hearing from God.
6. Worry kills your potential.
7. Worry, if you let it, can be a life master.

Worry is one of those things that bypasses the intellect and affects both the mind and the spirit. A lifestyle of worry will hinder a life of faith. To live worry-free is a choice. You don't have to worry about your life, about your home or about your future because God has already taken care of those things, so choose not to worry!

Proverbs 12:25 (NLT)

Worry weighs a person down; an encouraging word cheers a person up.

This is not an excuse for handling your finances in an immature manner or being flippant about life. This information arms you with the power of faith through the Word of God to make better life choices and become a person of faith. A believer in Christ should never be ruled by worry!

Here are some things we can do to help in the area of worry:

1. Read the Word. Proverbs is a great book to start with as it brings wisdom and understanding into your life.
2. Be accountable with your thought life. Take captive your thoughts and bring them under the subjection of Christ.
3. Pray every day. Specific prayers as opposed to general prayer times. When you pray, have a notebook with you so you can list out all the areas you need to see breakthrough in.
4. Listen to and obey your leaders. Your leaders look out for your best interests, so obeying their words of advice will help bring progress in your life. Beware that you don't get over-familiar with your leaders as it will destroy your ability to receive from them.
5. Take faith steps. The Bible tells us to walk by faith. We take steps forward, believing the next step to be where God wants us to be.
6. Be rooted in Church. Church is God's plan; to be outside of Church is to be outside of His plan and to forsake the power that is available to help you overcome.
7. Be a giver to the Church. Your four T's: Time, Talent, Treasure and Touch.
8. Guard your heart. This is very important: only let good seeds sink into your heart. Thoughts are like seeds; they will soon take root and grow, bearing fruit that will cause more problems in the future.
9. Keep a godly perspective in everything. A great comfort to anyone is knowing that in all things God is working for His good. No matter what is happening, God is working on your behalf and that brings a great perspective that produces peace.
10. Commit your ways to God. Talk over your plans and dreams with your pastors or leaders. This is not only wise but also biblical. Often your pastors and leaders can see things that you cannot see.

Philippians 4:5-7 (NIV)

Let your gentleness be evident to all. The Lord is near. Do not be anxious about anything, but in everything, by prayer and petition, with thanksgiving, present your requests to God. And the peace of God, which transcends all understanding, will guard your hearts and your minds in Christ Jesus.

My Prayer

Heavenly Father, I thank you for all the things you have done for me and for the many times you stepped in and rescued me from situations that I worried over. Father, I choose to let go and let you take control. Help me by your Word to be an overcomer in the name of Jesus. Amen!

God-Thoughts & Holy Spirit Promptings

_____

_____

_____

_____

_____

_____

_____

_____

_____

_____

_____

_____

God-Thoughts & Holy Spirit Promptings

_____

_____

_____

_____

_____

_____

_____

_____

_____

_____

_____

_____

An Extra Shot

(Chapter 33)
No Fear

Fear affects everyone. You cannot see it but you can surely feel it.
It can cause the most reserved and polite person to act
irrationally. On a recent flight back from the West Indies, the plane I
was on had just crossed over the Atlantic, flying at 38,000 feet, when
suddenly, without warning, it began to shake violently and drop,
swerving left and right. The overhead bins flew open and people were
being sick. It lasted for fifteen minutes or so and fear gripped
everyone on board. I started chatting to the young lady sitting next to
me as she was shaken up and very fearful. As we talked, I found out
that her dad was the pilot and she was flying for free. I said to her,
'Well, you don't need to worry; your dad has it under control!' To
which she replied, 'Yes, but I know him!' We are not meant to fear
man or things but fear the Lord!

1 Samuel 12:24 (NIV)

But be sure to fear the LORD and serve him faithfully with all your heart; consider what great things he has done for you.

We know that our Lord is not only our dad; He is our Father and will always be there to watch over us! There will always be tough times - crisis, poverty and challenges are all part of living on Earth - however, we don't need to worry or be overcome with fear; He is our Father and He knows what we need (Matthew 6: 24-33). All we have to do is let go and trust that he has everything under control.

Fear is always ready to reveal to us how inadequate we are, but remember, God is always with you! He will never leave you nor forsake you. When fear comes knocking on your door - whether it's sickness, family problems, money or some other crisis - remember that God is with you and He will never let harm come near you or those He loves. Answer the door in faith!

He is your Father and more than able to protect you. God has placed weapons in our hands so we can resist the enemy. These weapons are not carnal but mighty, pulling down strongholds and every vain imagination. Paul says it this way in Romans:

Romans 8:15 (NLT)

So you have not received a spirit that makes you fearful slaves. Instead, you received God's Spirit when he adopted you as his own children. Now we call him, "Abba, Father."

The Holy Spirit enables us to resist every fear, thought and action and turn it into faith. Here are some practical things we can do to overcome a lifestyle of fear:

1. Get into the Word. The Word of the Lord is part of our protective covering. When Jesus was tempted by the devil, He resisted

Satan by the Word. The Word helps us to stay rational and understand that He's got it all under control (Psalm 119).

2. Get into Church. When we are at Church, we are surrounded by people from the same local family who are more than able to walk with us, encourage us and pray with us. This is your true family. When we neglect Church, we turn off the power that is there to help us (Hebrews 10).

3. Get into the Spirit. We are to keep in step with the Spirit of God. The Spirit breathes life, strength and power. Through the power of the Holy Spirit we are able to dispel the works of darkness. By the power of the Holy Spirit we are able to lay hands on the sick and see them healed. His Spirit empowers us in times of weakness (Galatians 5).

Psalm 27:1-4 (NLT)

The LORD is my light and my salvation—so why should I be afraid? The LORD is my fortress, protecting me from danger, so why should I tremble? When evil people come to devour me, when my enemies and foes attack me, they will stumble and fall. Though a mighty army surrounds me, my heart will not be afraid. Even if I am attacked, I will remain confident. The one thing I ask of the LORD—the thing I seek most—is to live in the house of the LORD all the days of my life, delighting in the LORD's perfections and meditating in his Temple.

My Prayer

Father, I come against that spirit of fear. You have not given us a weak and feeble spirit, but a spirit that is strong and an overcomer. I commit all my ways to you. When situations come that bring fearful thoughts in my life I will stand on your Word and walk in faith that you are working on my behalf. Amen!

God-Thoughts & Holy Spirit Promptings

_____

_____

_____

_____

_____

_____

_____

_____

_____

_____

_____

_____

An Extra Shot

(Chapter 34)
Open Doors

Psalm 78:23 (NIV)

Yet he gave a command to the skies above and opened the doors of
the heavens.

Here is a question to provoke your thinking: *If you could
orchestrate your day, your week or your year, what would you
do differently?* I'm sure there are many things you could fill your
wish list with, but when it comes to your future it is not as mystical as
most would think.

Our futures are shaped mostly by choices. One of my sayings is that
'we are who we are today because of the choices we made yesterday.'
So, one of the ways I can shape my future is by making wiser and
better choices in my life. Another, more important way is by
partnering with a local church. Church is God's plan; to be outside of
Church is to be outside of His great plan for our lives.

Let's look at a few scriptures:

Genesis 4:7 (NLT)

> You will be accepted if you do what is right. But if you refuse to do what is right, then watch out! Sin is crouching at the door, eager to control you. But you must subdue it and be its master.

At every door in your life there's an opportunity for sin to take a foothold and stop you. The choices you make will determine if you master sin, or if sin masters you!

1 Corinthians 16:9 (NLT)

> There is a wide-open door for a great work here, although many oppose me.

At every wide-open door there will be opposition. Opposition can either stop you or strengthen you. For every door of sickness, God can open a door of healing; for every door of disappointment, God can open a reappointment; for every valley there is a mountain. He is God!

Don't quit at the first obstacle and don't stop because others think it's foolish. Many of the great inventions were laughed at by those who had no vision. *Note: Doors of faith seldom make any sense; this is why you have to trust God above calculations and budgets and take Him at His Word.*

One door you should always honour is the door of God's house. My wife and I resolved many years ago (before we held any position in Church) that we would never let anything stop us from being in God's house; not snow, or rain, or floods, or even a dead car! Why? To have a revelation of God means having a revelation of Church! Safety and life are found in His house, by being in His courts where His presence dwells. There are many things that can keep you from Church, but you should never choose to miss Church.

Matthew 7:7 (NIV)

Ask and it will be given to you; seek and you will find; knock and the door will be opened to you.

This is one of my favourite verses on open doors. It's not just down to what you physically do, but how you pray and position yourself in prayer. There are some doors you should shut, some doors you should open and some doors God will open for you. These doors become more discernable through a lifestyle of prayer. Prayer, coupled with fasting, makes a powerful tool for dealing with doors that just seem like they cannot be opened or cannot be closed.

Psalm 141:2-3 (NKJV)

Let my prayer be set before You as incense, The lifting up of my hands as the evening sacrifice. Set a guard, O LORD, over my mouth; Keep watch over the door of my lips.

My Prayer

Father, I come before you and ask that you help me to discern which doors are set before me. I pray that, through the power of your Holy Spirit, all unfruitful doors be shut and all doors of greatness for you and your Kingdom be opened. Amen!

God-Thoughts & Holy Spirit Promptings

_____

_____

_____

_____

_____

_____

_____

_____

_____

_____

_____

_____

An Extra Shot

(Chapter 35)

Power Up

2 Timothy 1:7 (NLT)

For God has not given us a spirit of fear and timidity, but of power, love, and self-discipline.

Fear can be really contagious. If you listen to fearful, negative reports for long enough you will end up believing them. I once heard a story of someone getting food poisoning from eating a bad hotdog at a baseball game in America. The medics asked that an announcement go out to all 20,000 people in the stadium, saying: '*If you have eaten a hot dog and feel sick, report to the front immediately.*' Around 5,000 people flooded to the front of the stadium as they all felt sick, and after a few hours it became an epidemic! Meanwhile, the original person who was sick had been treated by doctors who had soon realised that it was not food poisoning but severe heartburn! What caused all those people to feel sick? It was the announcement that went out telling them that if they had eaten a hotdog and felt sick to report to the front of the stadium! The hotdogs were fine; it was the suggestion that they may not have been that caused people to experience something that was not real.

We live in a time when there are many negative reports about the economy and the world we live in, but do you listen to them? Should you? Isaiah 53:1 asks the question, '*Whose report do you believe?*' Does this mean you ignore warnings of danger or impending trouble? No! You do, however, let God's Word be your ultimate source of power and light. The Message gives a great translation of an awesome scripture:

Psalm 119:105 (MSG)

By your words I can see where I'm going; they throw a beam of light on my dark path. I've committed myself and I'll never turn back from living by your righteous order. Everything's falling apart on me, GOD; put me together again with your Word. Festoon me with your finest sayings, GOD; teach me your holy rules. My life is as close as my own hands, but I don't forget what you have revealed. The wicked do their best to throw me off track, but I don't swerve an inch from your course. I inherited your book on living; it's mine forever— what a gift! And how happy it makes me! I concentrate on doing exactly what you say— I always have and always will.

We overcome fear by faith. Faith comes by hearing and hearing by the Word of the Lord (Romans 10:17). When fear raises its head let faith arise in you! Look how Paul puts it:

Romans 8:31-38 (NLT)

What shall we say about such wonderful things as these? If God is for us, who can ever be against us? Since he did not spare even his own Son but gave him up for us all, won't he also give us everything else? Who dares accuse us whom God has chosen for his own? No one—for God himself has given us right standing with himself. Who then will condemn us? No one—for Christ Jesus died for us and was raised to life for us, and he is sitting in the place of honour at God's right hand, pleading for us.

Can anything ever separate us from Christ's love? Does it mean he no longer loves us if we have trouble or calamity, or are persecuted, or hungry, or destitute, or in danger, or threatened with death? (As the Scriptures say, "For your sake we are killed every day; we are being slaughtered like sheep.") No, despite all these things, overwhelming victory is ours through Christ, who loved us. And I am convinced that nothing can ever separate us from God's love. Neither death nor life, neither angels nor demons, neither our fears for today nor our worries about tomorrow—not even the powers of hell can separate us from God's love.

Recently, I bought a satnav and it's great. Finding places and getting from A to B is a whole lot easier. But no matter how good it is, it needs to be powered up. It needs to be charged for it to work, which means my journey could be delayed by a lack of power. For us to get where God wants us to be, our spiritual batteries need to be charged up.

Practical ways to power up:

1. Remember that God loves you! Nothing builds our faith more than knowing in our hearts that God loves us. And there is nothing that can change that. No matter how much you've messed up, He still loves you!

2. Be in Church. No matter how tired you are, or how long your day has been, there is nothing like being in the house of God. Make a decision that you will always be in God's house!

3. Be a giver. Despite our current world crisis, we still sow, we still trust and we still give. If in need, plant a seed! Be faithful with your tithes, offerings and First Fruits. God will bless you!

4. Don't let go. It's easy to give up in the face of sickness, tiredness and struggle, but keep on fighting the fight of faith. Don't let go, your miracle is just around the corner! Your blessing will soon come; your mourning will be turned into dancing and your sorrow into joy. Don't give up! Winston Churchill once said, '*If you're going through Hell, just keep going!*'

5. Be a worshipper. Nothing charges our spiritual batteries like being in worship. Not just singing, but giving yourself to Him as a living sacrifice and worshipping Him in spirit and in truth.

Psalm 91 (MSG)

You who sit down in the High God's presence, spend the night in Shaddai's shadow, Say this: "GOD, you're my refuge. I trust in you and I'm safe!" That's right—he rescues you from hidden traps, shields you from deadly hazards. His huge outstretched arms protect you— under them you're perfectly safe; his arms fend off all harm. Fear nothing—not wild wolves in the night, not flying arrows in the day, Not disease that prowls through the darkness, not disaster that erupts at high noon. Even though others succumb all around, drop like flies right and left, no harm will even graze you. You'll stand untouched, watch it all from a distance, watch the wicked turn into corpses. Yes, because GOD's your refuge, the High God your very own home, Evil can't get close to you, harm can't get through the door. He ordered his angels to guard you wherever you go. If you stumble, they'll catch you; their job is to keep you from falling. You'll walk unharmed among lions and snakes, and kick young lions and serpents from the path. "If you'll hold on to me for dear life," says GOD, "I'll get you out of any trouble. I'll give you the best of care if you'll only get to know and trust me. Call me and I'll answer, be at your side in bad times; I'll rescue you, then throw you a party. I'll give you a long life, give you a long drink of salvation!"

My Prayer

Today, I ask for a fresh filling of your Holy Spirit. I ask, Holy Spirit, come and invade all of my life! I ask that you give me strength to overcome. When I feel weak, through you I become strong. Father, remind me, by your Holy Spirit, of the truth and principles of your Word. Amen!

God-Thoughts & Holy Spirit Promptings

_____

_____

_____

_____

_____

_____

_____

_____

_____

_____

_____

_____

God-Thoughts & Holy Spirit Promptings

_____

_____

_____

_____

_____

_____

_____

_____

_____

_____

_____

_____

(Chapter 36)
Where Did I Put It?

Psalm 56:3 (NLT)

But when I am afraid, I will put my trust in you.

If we are honest we'll say 'Yes, I have certain fears,' and 'Yes, I do worry'. Fear and worry are not meant to be a condemnation in themselves, however *living* in fear and worry is wrong and is actually a sin. There are many things that can test our trust in God - things like sickness, the future, finances and many more - and they can bring sleepless nights and distractions; however, they should only act as a reminder to put our trust in the Lord.

Psalm 20:7 (CEV)

Some people trust the power of chariots or horses, but we trust you, LORD God.

God is our Father; He only has good thoughts towards His children. Psalm 91 provides great comfort for those who worry and are fearful.

Psalm 91:14-16 (NLT)

The LORD says, "I will rescue those who love me. I will protect those who trust in my name. When they call on me, I will answer; I will be with them in trouble. I will rescue and honour them. I will reward them with a long life and give them my salvation."

Seven "I will's" from the Lord (taken from Psalm 91:14-16):

1. I will rescue those who love me.
2. I will protect those who trust in my name.
3. I will answer them.
4. I will be with them in times of trouble.
5. I will honour them.
6. I will reward them with long life.
7. I will give them my salvation.

What great promises from the Lord! When the temptation of fear and worry comes knocking on your door, what do you do? The choice you make shows one of two things: either you put your trust in God or choose to work it out your own way.

Some people seek sympathy more than the Lord. They always have a problem or sickness to talk about, and if it's not to do with them, it's to do with their children or their workplace, or maybe a situation with their husband or wife. By focusing on these things they fail to remain focused on the Lord and His promises. They seek sympathy over the Lord. Here are some truths about sympathy:

1. Sympathy has no power to change your situation.
2. Sympathy cannot heal.
3. Sympathy cannot provide.
4. Sympathy gives temporary comfort.
5. Sympathy is based on emotion and does not change the facts.
6. Sympathy shifts your focus from the Lord and on to man.

Put your trust in the Lord. Do not let ungodly emotions rule you and don't let sickness rob you. Pick yourself up in the Lord and He will come through for you!

Psalm 52:8-9 (NLT)

But I am like an olive tree, thriving in the house of God. I will always trust in God's unfailing love. I will praise you forever, O God, for what you have done. I will trust in your good name in the presence of your faithful people.

My Prayer

Father, today I will put my trust in you! I know that you are for me and that brings such strength in me. I will read your Word, I will pray and I will seek you. Thank you for the gifts of the Holy Spirit and your Church that help me to be strong when I am weak. I will trust in you at all times. Amen!

God-Thoughts & Holy Spirit Promptings

_____

_____

_____

_____

_____

_____

_____

_____

_____

_____

_____

An Extra Shot

(Chapter 37)

Slow Down

James 1:19 (NLT)

Understand this, my dear brothers and sisters: You must all be quick to listen, slow to speak, and slow to get angry.

The things that get us into the most trouble are our words; whether it's something we have said or sent in a text or email in the heat of the moment. Words are like wild horses, once they get out it's very hard to catch them! The Bible gives us many words of wisdom that can help us with everyday life. The book of Proverbs helps us with life's choices, particularly with making better choices so we enjoy life. When we are put in a predicament or tough situation we should never answer out of anger, as in many circumstances it can lead to disappointment and regret.

Psalm 19:14 (NIV)

May the words of my mouth and the meditation of my heart be pleasing in your sight, O LORD, my Rock and my Redeemer.

The Holy Spirit is given as our comforter, our guide and our source of strength. He helps us in the moments when life gets too 'big' for us, when life brings a situation out of the blue that pins us down or something happens that knocks the wind out of our sails. He brings to remembrance the right words and thoughts that encourage us and help to turn around a bad situation for good.

> ### John 14:26 (NKJV)
>
> But the Helper, the Holy Spirit, whom the Father will send in My name, He will teach you all things, and bring to your remembrance all things that I said to you.

Pausing is one of the most neglected responses in everyday life. Fewer problems occur when we slow down or pause and think very carefully before taking any action. This may mean pausing before you send that text or reply to that email! When we mix actions with unchecked emotions, problems can soon come our way.

Jesus was one hundred percent man as well as one hundred percent God. He had all the feelings and emotions of a human being, yet He showed us by His example that although He had emotions, emotions never had Him. Through the help and guidance of the Holy Spirit, God's grace helps us in times of weakness. When life gets busy and the world seems to be getting on top of you, take heart because Christ overcame this world!

Seven things to do in moments of uncertainty:

1. Nothing! Often, just waiting a while and sleeping on it brings a clearer picture of the situation.
2. Pray. Prayer is our greatest weapon; Jesus prayed, so we too ought to pray (Philippians 4:6-7).
3. Listen to the Holy Spirit. The Holy Spirit is our source and guide, our comforter and the one who reminds us of scriptural truth (John 15 & 16).

4. Get to Church. Church is God's plan. When you're in Church you are surrounded by a spiritual family that can help bring godly direction and wisdom (Hebrews 10:25).

5. Read the Word. The Word of the Lord is a lamp unto our feet; in other words it illuminates the dark places and uncertain areas of our lives (Psalm 119).

6. Seek pastoral help. The elders, pastors and leaders of the Church are there to be a help and guide. Obedience to their wisdom always brings reward. It may not feel that way initially, but if you listen, you will reap the fruits of that obedience (Hebrews 13:17; Proverbs 12:1).

7. Trust God. Sometimes the only thing we can do is to trust God. Let go and put all things into His hands. Remember, He is your Father who only wants the best for you (Proverbs 3:4-6).

John 16:33 (NIV)

"I have told you these things, so that in me you may have peace. In this world you will have trouble. But take heart! I have overcome the world."

My Prayer

Father, help me to be a person who waits on you, to take things a bit slower and not be rash in my decision-making. By your Word as my guide and as a filter of truth, I pray that I will not be ruled by ungodly emotions but by the Holy Spirit. Amen!

God-Thoughts & Holy Spirit Promptings

_____

_____

_____

_____

_____

_____

_____

_____

_____

_____

_____

_____

(Chapter 38)
Up

Exodus 35:22 (NLT)

Both men and women came, all whose hearts were willing. They brought to the LORD their offerings of gold - broaches, earrings, rings from their fingers, and necklaces. They presented gold objects of every kind as a special offering to the LORD.

Giving and Christianity go together. The Bible tells us that God so loved the world He gave His only Son (John 3:16), so you can see that because God loved the world, He gave. We, as God's people, should be the most generous people on the planet. We should not be stingy, greedy, or self-promoting, but true representatives of Christ. This is seen first of all by how we give to the Lord. Giving is attractive to God and He takes it very seriously. When we give to God it should be our best and not what is left over; God gave His son, His best!

Genesis 4:3-5 (NLT)

When it was time for the harvest, Cain presented some of his crops as a gift to the LORD. Abel also brought a gift—the best of the firstborn lambs from his flock. The LORD accepted Abel and his gift, but he did not accept Cain and his gift. This made Cain very angry, and he looked dejected.

When we give our best to God, we always receive God's best in return. In the Old Testament, when an offering was brought to the Lord it was burnt and the aroma went up to Heaven as a sweet savour that was pleasing to the Lord.

Genesis 8:21 (NASB)

The LORD smelled the soothing aroma; and the LORD said to Himself, "I will never again curse the ground on account of man, for the intent of man's heart is evil from his youth; and I will never again destroy every living thing, as I have done."

We don't bring those types of offerings today; instead we bring our money to the Lord's house in the form of tithes, offerings and First Fruits. These are received by the Lord in the same way; obedience always brings blessing. When we bring our tithes (the ten percent of our income which belongs to the Lord), our offerings and our First Fruits, we are attracting the favour of God on us. We are not buying God's favour but attracting God through our lifestyle of faith.

Our tithe represents our first action, the first portion to the Lord. If the first part is holy and blessed then the rest is holy and blessed. Some say that it does not matter what you give as long as you have a good heart - well, that is wrong and it does matter, a lot! Whenever we bring an offering to the Lord's house it should be a sacrifice.

Once, when I was in India, I heard a story about a village that was making animal sacrifices. The local eagles learnt to scavenge from the meat on the altar. Once, during a sacrifice, an eagle swooped down and grabbed a piece of meat and in the process took a live coal in its grip. The eagle flew to its nest and dropped the meat to the chicks, along with the live coal. Sadly, the nest, the tree and half of the forest was destroyed by fire, started by the coal. So it is when we take what belongs to God; we destroy our surroundings and our future.

Mark 12:41-45 (NLT)

Jesus sat down near the collection box in the Temple and watched as the crowds dropped in their money. Many rich people put in large amounts. Then a poor widow came and dropped in two small coins. Jesus called his disciples to him and said, "I tell you the truth, this poor widow has given more than all the others who are making contributions. For they gave a tiny part of their surplus, but she, poor as she is, has given everything she had to live on."

Notice that it was not the amount that Jesus was interested in but the one who gave her all. The widow gave all she had left to live on; this was a true sacrifice. What occurs to me as well is that out of all the places Jesus could have been He chose to show up during the offering and watch how people gave. Giving is important to God. We should always give to God that which costs us something.

2 Samuel 24:24 (NLT)

But the king (David) replied to Araunah, "No, I insist on buying it, for I will not present burnt offerings to the LORD my God that have cost me nothing." So David paid him fifty pieces of silver for the threshing floor and the oxen.

David understood the principle of giving to God that which is truly a sacrifice. He could have got it all for free, but David knew the Lord and chose to give to Him only what cost him something.

Psalm 50:14 (Amp)

Offer to God the sacrifice of thanksgiving, and pay your vows to the Most High.

My Prayer

Father, I will bring my tithe and offerings to you faithfully. I resist any negative thoughts or feelings that will stop me from bringing my first and best to you. I know you give far more than I could ever give to you. I pray that as I do this, your windows will be open over my life and your blessings will surround me. Amen!

God-Thoughts & Holy Spirit Promptings

_____

_____

_____

_____

_____

_____

_____

_____

_____

_____

_____

God-Thoughts & Holy Spirit Promptings

_____

_____

_____

_____

_____

_____

_____

_____

_____

_____

_____

_____

An Extra Shot

(Chapter 39)
Peace, Man

John 16:33 (NLT)

"I have told you all this so that you may have peace in me. Here on earth you will have many trials and sorrows. But take heart, because I have overcome the world."

The joyful, satisfied believers' life comes by faith. What do I mean? Well, not every day will be a blessed day; some days will be full of trials, hardship, sorrow and disappointment. What do we do when our world turns upside down? This is where faith comes in. True faith causes us to seek God first and not let our problems overshadow Him.

Psalm 121:1-2 (NLT)

I look up to the mountains does my help come from there? My help comes from the LORD, who made heaven and earth!

Notice in this text that you have to raise your eyes a little higher and look over that mountain to find the Creator waiting for you. The truth is that God doesn't always wipe away our mountains. Yes, He is the Lord that heals, but good, Bible-living believers still die of sicknesses. In these very tough times we should draw closer to God - by faith! Don't fall into the temptation of staying on your own, alone, trying to work things out by yourself. Get up and get into the house of God. It may be hard to face people and see others enjoying the day but you have to raise yourself above the situation, above the mountain, and look to the Lord. He will give you the strength to overcome. There is a season to mourn but also a season to rejoice!

2 Samuel 12:19-23 (NLT)

When David saw them whispering, he realized what had happened. "Is the child dead?" he asked. "Yes," they replied, "he is dead." Then David got up from the ground, washed himself, put on lotions, and changed his clothes. He went to the Tabernacle and worshipped the LORD. After that, he returned to the palace and was served food and ate. His advisers were amazed. "We don't understand you," they told him. "While the child was still living, you wept and refused to eat. But now that the child is dead, you have stopped your mourning and are eating again."

David replied, "I fasted and wept while the child was alive, for I said, 'Perhaps the LORD will be gracious to me and let the child live.' But why should I fast when he is dead? Can I bring him back again? I will go to him one day, but he cannot return to me."

In the world today - and equally in the Christian life - there are some incorrect mentalities, especially when it comes to faith and blessing. We can sometimes associate faith with blessing, healing, provision and always having a great testimony of overcoming. Yes, God will bless you; yes, He can heal you, and yes, you will overcome - however, you have to trust God 'that all things will work together for good'.

I am always moved by Hebrews 11. It is awesome and inspiring to read how all these people of faith did incredible things, but if you take the time to read the entire text you will see that not all overcame, were rescued or raised from the dead.

Hebrews 11:35b-39 (NLT)

But others were tortured, refusing to turn from God in order to be set free. They placed their hope in a better life after the resurrection. Some were jeered at, and their backs were cut open with whips. Others were chained in prisons. Some died by stoning, some were sawed in half, and others were killed with the sword. Some went about wearing skins of sheep and goats, destitute and oppressed and mistreated. They were too good for this world, wandering over deserts and mountains, hiding in caves and holes in the ground. All these people earned a good reputation because of their faith, yet none of them received all that God had promised.

It's in these times that we apply faith and let the peace of God cover us. Paul, in his last letter before being beheaded, wrote these life-changing words. Apply these words and thoughts to your life today.

Philippians 4:4-7 (NLT)

Always be full of joy in the Lord. I say it again—rejoice! Let everyone see that you are considerate in all you do. Remember, the Lord is coming soon. Don't worry about anything; instead, pray about everything. Tell God what you need, and thank him for all he has done. Then you will experience God's peace, which exceeds anything we can understand. His peace will guard your hearts and minds as you live in Christ Jesus.

My Prayer

Father, I will trust you with all my heart, regardless of what I receive or how I feel. I thank you for this peace that is in my life because of you. I will not worry, fret or be uneasy. I love your leading and know you have my future in your hands, and this brings the greatest peace in my life. Thank you! Amen!

God-Thoughts & Holy Spirit Promptings

_____

_____

_____

_____

_____

_____

_____

_____

_____

_____

_____

_____

(Chapter 40)

His Audacious Plan

Jeremiah 29:11 (NLT)

"For I know the plans I have for you," says the LORD. "They are plans for good and not for disaster, to give you a future and a hope."

Planning ahead makes for stress-free living most of the time. Planning is a good thing (like planning before a trip, making sure you have your passport, visa, cash, contacts, etc.), but even with the best laid plans and most thorough check-lists, situations can still go wrong and cause stress and worry.

When it comes to God, however, His plans are always good and stress-free. This fulfilling life depends on one word: *trust*. To have a stress-free and successful Christian life, trust is essential. We need to learn to trust in God with all, daily in everything and every situation. It never ceases to amaze me when I think about the grace that God uses when He calls each one of us. I know for a fact that if it was up to me, I wouldn't choose me! But God, in His wisdom and grace, decided before time to choose us and call us into His Kingdom.

Jeremiah 1:5 (NLT)

"I knew you before I formed you in your mother's womb. Before you were born I set you apart and appointed you... to the nations."

Not only did He choose us, He appointed us for something great. His plan may seem ridiculous or even audacious, but we trust that God's great plan will come to pass in our lives. With this awesome Word, we stand up in His grace and proclaim with a loud voice: 'No weapon formed against me shall prosper! I am a child of God! I am blessed to be a blessing!'

Now, these things only happen because of God's grace and His ability to forgive us and see beyond our weaknesses and flaws. This is why we can say, like the Apostle Paul, 'Yet, in all these things we are more than conquerors!' The ability to stand, to fight and to press on in God comes from reflecting on the cross of Christ and remembering what Jesus did for us.

Romans 8:36-45 (NLT)

(As the Scriptures say, "For your sake we are killed every day; we are being slaughtered like sheep.") No, despite all these things, overwhelming victory is ours through Christ, who loved us. And I am convinced that nothing can ever separate us from God's love. Neither death nor life, neither angels nor demons, neither our fears for today nor our worries about tomorrow—not even the powers of hell can separate us from God's love. No power in the sky above or in the earth below—indeed, nothing in all creation will ever be able to separate us from the love of God that is revealed in Christ Jesus our Lord.

Storms will come in life, despite all our plans and attempts to avoid them. The issue is not the actual storm but the reason behind it. If God knows the beginning from the end, then He knows every storm that is coming our way before it begins to blow. Why do we go through storms? Well, some storms are a result of our own disobedience and our own bad choices. Other storms help us to learn what it means to trust in God. Storms help us to stand strong, storms teach us to hold on and storms draw us closer to God. That is God's ultimate plan; that as He draws us closer to Him, we will come. It may seem audacious, but that's His plan!

Psalm 121 (NLT)

I look up to the mountains does my help come from there? My help comes from the LORD, who made heaven and earth! He will not let you stumble; the one who watches over you will not slumber. Indeed, he who watches over Israel never slumbers or sleeps. The LORD himself watches over you! The LORD stands beside you as your protective shade. The sun will not harm you by day, nor the moon at night. The LORD keeps you from all harm and watches over your life. The LORD keeps watch over you as you come and go, both now and forever.

My Prayer

Father, thank you for choosing me to be a part of your awesome Kingdom. Help me make the daily adjustments and choices to fall into your will and future for my life. You are a big, strong and loving God. I place my future into your hands. Amen!

God-Thoughts & Holy Spirit Promptings

_____

_____

_____

_____

_____

_____

_____

_____

_____

_____

_____

_____

(Chapter 41)
A Great Recipe

> **Proverbs 9:10 (NLT)**
>
> Fear of the LORD is the foundation of wisdom. Knowledge of the Holy One results in good judgment.

Every great dish calls for great ingredients, and so it is with life. An enjoyable life needs a good recipe to make it happen and it never comes by chance! The book of Proverbs gives us the ingredients to help us make an enjoyable life. Here are the two foundational ingredients: wisdom and understanding (or good judgement).

Failure to learn from past failures only results in future failures! Wisdom and good judgement will make the simple wise and help you avoid failure in life. God's Word is such that anyone who lives it and applies it sees great blessings.

> **Psalm 19:7-11 (NLT)**
>
> The instructions of the LORD are perfect, reviving the soul. The decrees of the LORD are trustworthy, making wise the simple. The commandments of the LORD are right, bringing joy to the heart.

> The commands of the LORD are clear; giving insight for living. Reverence for the LORD is pure, lasting forever. The laws of the LORD are true; each one is fair. They are more desirable than gold, even the finest gold. They are sweeter than honey, even honey dripping from the comb. They are a warning to your servant, a great reward for those who obey them.

The ability to make wise choices will bring many rewards. Choices come with different levels of consequences; some are small, others great. Wisdom, guided by the Word and His Holy Spirit, results in great choices. Offence is a choice - choose not to get offended. Forgiveness is also a choice - choose to forgive. Developing good judgement will help you choose correctly.

Christ is our example; there were times when He chose to get angry with others and times He chose to show kindness and forgiveness. Sometimes trouble comes our way because of what we say. Remember the example of Jesus, who kept quiet when questioned by Pilate. You need to learn when to keep quiet as it will save your life!

Proverbs 10:19 (NLT)

> Too much talk leads to sin. Be sensible and keep your mouth shut.

Not only is it wise to guard your tongue but also your eyes. If your eyes go where Jesus can't, then you're watching the wrong thing. We are to fix our eyes on what God asks us to. Keep your gaze locked straight ahead and be on guard for things that could distract you.

This was the covenant that Job made with the Lord:

Job 31:1 (NIV)

> I made a covenant with my eyes not to look lustfully at a girl *(or however it applies to you! - author)*

The greatest guidance and strength we can get is found in Church and comes from being under the direction of the senior leaders of the house. Here are four questions for you to ponder:

1. Are you in Church whenever you should be? You should never choose to miss Church (Hebrews 10:25).
2. Do you as a parent make sure your kids are in Church when they should be? Sometimes it's easy to fail to lead correctly in the home by not encouraging your children (especially teens) to be in Church. Do you see Church as a priority in their lives or as something they do once they are free from everything else?
3. Do you react or respond to correction and discipline? No one enjoys being corrected or disciplined, but there are very good reasons for it. When correction and discipline are done in a godly manner, they lead to a better life in the long term (Proverbs 12).
4. Are you a person of wisdom and understanding? How you answer the above questions will determine whether or not you are a person of wisdom and discernment. What happens in your heart will determine the direction of your life. Be wise, listen and follow the ways of the Lord. It will save your life and the lives of your kids.

Proverbs 3:1-6 (NLT)

My child, never forget the things I have taught you. Store my commands in your heart. If you do this, you will live many years, and your life will be satisfying. Never let loyalty and kindness leave you! Tie them around your neck as a reminder. Write them deep within your heart. Then you will find favour with both God and people, and you will earn a good reputation. Trust in the Lord with all your heart; do not depend on your own understanding. Seek his will in all you do, and he will show you which path to take.

My Prayer

Father, I ask for wisdom and understanding. You said in your Word that 'anyone who asks for wisdom, you will give it generously,' let wisdom be in my life so I may make great choices and show great discernment every day. You are my rock and strength, oh Lord. Keep my foot from stumbling like the fool. Amen!

God-Thoughts & Holy Spirit Promptings

_____

_____

_____

_____

_____

_____

_____

_____

_____

_____

_____

God-Thoughts & Holy Spirit Promptings

_____

_____

_____

_____

_____

_____

_____

_____

_____

_____

_____

_____

An Extra Shot

(Chapter 42)
No Worries

Matthew 6:34 (NLT)

"So don't worry about tomorrow, for tomorrow will bring its own worries. Today's trouble is enough for today."

There are so many things that can cause us to worry. Life can be a breeding ground for the many seeds of worry. Worry, unchecked, will lead to discouragement and discouragement, unchecked, can lead to depression. On a recent trip we had the worry of when we would fly home! This can lead to lots of problems naturally but also emotionally which, unchecked, can lead to doubts like 'Should I ever fly again? What if it happens again? I don't want a repeat of last time!' These things (and many others!) are out of our control and worry cannot solve the problem. All we can do is trust that God will take care of us.

Matthew 6:27 (NLT)

Can all your worries add a single moment to your life?

Jesus tells us not to worry, so worrying is something we should not do! We are not to worry about our life, our health or our future; all we are called to do is trust that our Heavenly Father has all our cares in the palm of His hand. Now, this doesn't mean we don't do our part - looking after ourselves, paying our bills on time, etc. - we must do what we can and God will do the rest. But in moments when your world has been jolted by unforeseen circumstances you are not to worry, instead you should pray!

Philippians 4:6-7 (NLT)

Don't worry about anything; instead, pray about everything. Tell God what you need, and thank him for all he has done. Then you will experience God's peace, which exceeds anything we can understand. His peace will guard your hearts and minds as you live in Christ Jesus.

When we worry we limit God, stopping Him from doing what He said he would do. Worry has a way of causing us to take our eyes off of the Lord and focus on the problems instead. When we worry we can lose sleep, we weaken in faith and the enemy can sprinkle seeds of fear and doubt in our hearts. We need to remember that the perfect love which God has for us casts out all outlandish thoughts and fears!

The love of God is proof enough that He will take care of all our needs. I am inspired by the words of Shadrach, Meshach, and Abednego: 'Our God is able to rescue us from your power, but even if He does not, we will never serve your gods!' (Daniel 3: 16-18). No worries!

So, do you worry? Does worry have a stronghold in your life? If so, then today, when worry comes knocking on your door, answer it in faith. The love of God helps us to deal with fear and worry.

1 John 4:17-18 (MSG)

God is love. When we take up permanent residence in a life of love, we live in God and God lives in us. This way, love has the run of the house, becomes at home and mature in us, so that we're free of worry on Judgment Day—our standing in the world is identical with Christ's. There is no room in love for fear. Well-formed love banishes fear. Since fear is crippling, a fearful life—fear of death, fear of judgment—is one not yet fully formed in love.

Ten commands for when uncertainty comes:

1. Stop and pray.
2. Hold on to His Word.
3. Daily be filled with the Holy Spirit.
4. Grace and mercy must be fresh every day.
5. Don't worry; it's a sin to worry.
6. Take captive every carnal thought and make it obedient to God's Word.
7. Get to Church, worship Him during the storm.
8. Read your Bible every day.
9. Give to the Lord your tithes and offerings.
10. Celebrate and share testimonies about God's goodness.

My Prayer

Father, I'm sorry for the times I spend worrying. I ask for your forgiveness. From today, I will spend more time in your Word, more time in prayer and less time trying to work things out myself. Into your hands I commit my life. I know that you love me and that all things are in your hands. Amen!

God-Thoughts & Holy Spirit Promptings

_____

_____

_____

_____

_____

_____

_____

_____

_____

_____

_____

_____

Also from Harvest City Publishing

Partnership Guide
Chip Kawalsingh
2007, ISBN 978-0-9549580-9-1

The *Partnership Guide* was written as a membership course for Harvest City Church. However, because of the timeless truths and principles, this book can be used for new converts as well as young leadership training sessions in any country. Harvest City Church has experienced steady growth with a large committed membership due to these lessons being taught in 17 sessions.

Formation Leadership
Chip Kawalsingh
2006, ISBN 978-0-9549580-6-0

Building and maintaining a great team is no easy task. Even people who lead great teams will tell you they have difficulty getting the leaders to think alike. *Formation Leadership* is written as part of a leadership development series in which both young and mature leaders alike can be taught the heart of a senior pastor.

This book comprises a series of seminars where the heart and spiritual DNA of the senior pastors can be transferred to those who are called to leadership. Leaders need to be developed in their understanding of the 'how to' of church life. This book provides the answers, along with the attitudes, that anyone can use to springboard their leadership team into formation.

Find out more and order online at harvestcitypublishing.com

Also from Harvest City Publishing

God, a Mocha & Me
Chip Kawalsingh
2009, ISBN 978-0-9561415-0-7

God, a Mocha & Me aims to provide a series of short life lessons to help believers everywhere delve deeply into the Word of God on various issues.

The believer's greatest need is to spend time with God, pray effectively, read the Word and hear from Him about what to do in life.

God, a Mocha & Me helps the believer access the heart of God through His Word - anytime, anywhere - to lay the foundations for a highly successful life.

Keys To Building A Great Church
Cooper, De Jong, Tose, Kawalsingh, Sakellariou
2009, ISBN 978-0-9561415-1-4

"How can we build a great church?" is a question that is asked by church leaders probably more than any other, and is probably the hardest to answer fully. This book has been written as a resource for leaders, to pass on the experience and wisdom gained by the authors over many years of service in God's Kingdom and in building His Church, in the hope of answering that question.

Find out more and order online at harvestcitypublishing.com

Further Recommendation

This book is so practical for everyday living, you would think the author had personal insight into your life and thoughts. He gives the problem which affects us all and then he gives the antidote. Then rather than lose the challenge given, through time and forgetfulness, he encourages the reader to write down in the blank spaces the thoughts and actions that we should work on.

Chip has an amazing revelation of God's incredible plan called 'Church' which comes out regularly in these chapters. This book has something for church members, women, men, youth, married people, older people, leaders and pastors; something for everyone, no matter what circumstances or situation we are in. Not only does it help in practical ways, but also refreshes our spirit and teaches us how to walk closer to our Lord Jesus.

Thank you, Chip, for another excellent tool to help us all. A book well done.

Colin Cooper
Senior Pastor, Huddersfield Christian Fellowship
Chairman, Ministers Fellowship Europe